The We.piranha

The First Installment, Volume 1

Shena Blueggel

Published by Shena Blueggel, 2025.

THE WE.PIRANHA

First edition. May 28, 2025.

ISBN: 979-8227209993

Written by Shena Blueggel.

Table of Contents

Evil walks in the shadows of lies and deceit, in the darkness—the We.piranha lives!

—Introduction—

The We.piranha, AKA the piranha, on one hand a tactical military dream, on the other hand a psychological nightmare. The piranha is the ultimate—God—device. A device rocked with evil by trolls and hackers alike. Powerful sentiment exploits no man should have such power, yet the piranha gives one man all the power in the world.

This book is dedicated to the victims of the We.piranha. The intention is to guide individuals through some of the steps they can take, as well as some of the steps I have taken, to attempt a mass piranha eradication. Aspirations of a piranha-free life bring hope and must not be lost. It is possible to eradicate this parasite—very difficult, but possible. A lesser, more abrupt approach is to alleviate the pain of the piranha through abrasive measures.

The We.piranha has been haunting, and tormenting, me for over five years now. I do not know everything about the We.piranha, hence by writing this book, I hope to help others in a way no one was able to help me.

My wife and I live in the Western United States. Life stays simple—chickens, goats, and an occasional glass of Moscato. We keep our internet and all our devices extremely simple as well. For my safety, I will not be listing make or model of any devices, as this could jeopardize my well-being and progress with this common problem. I have a couple televisions, phones, tablets, computers, modem and router. Essentially, all the basic stuff. Regrettably, the piranha takes our simple life and perplexes our way of existence.

The biggest problem with the We.piranha is its omnipresence. The piranha leeches to every device, everywhere. The possibilities to cause harm are always elaborate and never-ending with the piranha. As many devices you believe it has infiltrated, the number is likely higher. This is the beginning of the journey.

—Chapter 1—

Start by approaching your specific situation with the belief the We.piranha is more intelligent than any device you own. Unfortunate to say, but it is more intelligent—much more intelligent. In order to have a chance at beating the We.piranha, you need to think old school! Take your complex setup, and un-complex it!

This is the only way to attempt to get on even battlegrounds. Except you are never going to be on even battlegrounds with the piranha. Regrettably, no matter what you or I do, we will always be at a disadvantage. Knowing this we must use everything at our disposal, to our advantage. Do not take anything for granted when fighting the piranha, and be creative.

First, we must breakdown what the We.piranha generally offers for the troll/ hacker.

1. **Wi-Fi Interception**—The We.piranha is capable of detecting and intercepting Wi-Fi signals. It can scan for Wi-Fi networks operating in specific frequencies, typically within the 2.4 GHz and 5 GHz bands, and analyze the traffic passing through these networks. This may include data such as email messages or other unencrypted information sent over the network.

2. **Packet Capture**—The We.piranha may capture data packets traveling over the Wi-Fi network. This can help intercept, and analyze, both encrypted and unencrypted traffic. Depending on the sophistication of the device, it likely possesses the capability to break certain encryption protocols, or at least extract metadata such as device identifiers, network activity, and communication patterns.

3. **Surveillance Capabilities**—The We.piranha can be used in covert, surveillance operations, enabling operators to monitor communications in real-time. It may have capabilities to work passively without alerting the target system, making it suitable for tactical operations in sensitive environments.

4. Location Tracking—The We.piranha can also be used to track the physical location of devices actively transmitting over Wi-Fi networks. This is achieved by measuring signal strength direction and triangulating the position of a Wi-Fi device based on its signal transmission.

5. Tactical Use—In a military or security context, these sensors are valuable for monitoring enemy communications, or conducting operations to disable or disrupt adversary networks. It may also be used for preventing data, leaks, or identifying unauthorized devices within a secured perimeter.

6. Countermeasures—The We.piranha does include tools to help detect and counteract the use of encrypted or hidden Wi-Fi networks. The We.piranha also includes features to jam or disrupt Wi-Fi communication within a specified area.

Overall, the We.piranha is a sophisticated tool intended for monitoring and intercepting wireless communications in a variety of applications, from tactical military operations to intelligence gathering and law enforcement surveillance. Nevertheless, specifics of the We.piranha may vary depending on its intended purpose, capabilities, and design features, which are usually proprietary and kept confidential due to security concerns by the troll/hacker. The key point, never underestimate the hacker nor the piranha.

Important to emphasize at this point, the piranha does have the capability of utilizing Voice Over Internet Protocol, AKA VOIP. Technically speaking, the troll/hacker is transferring phone calls from voice into digital signal. This gives the troll the ability to eavesdrop on phone calls.

Lastly, do not rule out extenders and other devices attached to the piranha; they make it even more powerful and dangerous.

On paper, the We.piranha appears mysterious or cryptic, but witnessing it in action takes it to a whole new level.

—Chapter 2—

The main devices I have encountered, of the We.piranha, are the We.piranha.xb6 and the We.piranha.off; other versions—with other names do exist, and they always contain the word piranha. Keep an extreme—open mind—to this idea as it will likely come into play for you, as it has for me. Such goes the saying—knowledge is power. The more known about these piranha versions, the better! As far as my knowledge goes, all of these piranhas are the same. They are all used in the same manner, meant for the same functions, and have the exact same capabilities. The advancement of the hacker controls the advancement of the We.piranha.

Research implies the We.piranha has been described as many things and/or names—Master installation device for Xfinity and/or Comcast, Mesh Backhaul GRE(Generic Routing Encapsulation), Backbone, Presidential/ Secret Service device, Tactical device made by Pegasus Intelligence, Israeli Interception Kit, and the Ukrainian Piranha AVD 360. It is probable there are also other versions/names of the piranha out there in the wild. This whole situation, or conversation—involving the piranha—is such a hidden and mythical topic; I absolutely believe other versions/names are out there in the wild.

The primary challenge with narrowing down the exact name is no one truly knows the exact name. Nevertheless, as stated it always has the word piranha in the name somewhere. Subsequently, the only individuals whom seem to know, the true name and full nature of the device, are the trolls and hackers engaged in these malevolent acts against us all.

From all known knowledge, the We.piranha(this version of the piranha) origination was a collaboration between the engineers working for Xfinity/ Comcast and a private tactical organization known as Pegasus Intelligence. The design and build were nothing short of brilliant. Pegasus Intelligence is a technology company specializing in creating solutions for field service management. Basically, the We.piranha is intended to help technicians efficiently manage a variety of tasks, whilst in the field, and has played a significant role in improving the efficiency of Xfinity/Comcast service installations.

This lab-created(piranha) version seems to be the origin of the We.piranha; however, other—less sophisticated—versions predate the We.piranha. On the flipside, other versions most likely postdate the We.piranha as well.

When all is said and done, no matter what name it is given, to my basic understanding, they are all the same device; do not be fooled. A pseudonym(a fake name), metonymy(using a related term), or simply renaming the We.piranha will not hoodwink us. We can call the piranha a fish, but to us, it is still just a hacking device. Do not let anyone—ever—persuade you otherwise. The We.piranha is exactly what you think it is. We must take a deeper dive into each of these piranha names to fully understand the etymology.

1. Master installation device for Xfinity and/or Comcast—When someone does not have internet and needs a connection, the installers bring out a master device. One of these devices is known as the Gateway Piranha, AKA the We.piranha, although this model has since been discontinued. The Xfinity/Comcast worker—whom illegally acquired this device—left the company in 2018, taking it with him. Subsequently, there are many of these installation devices, physical and virtual, still roaming around—in the wild—today! Note— whether internet or cell phone, the whole time whilst battling the We.piranha, I have been an Xfinity/Comcast customer.

2. Mesh Backhaul GRE(Generic Routing Encapsulation)—Essentially this transports data traffic between a local access network, such as what Xfinity/Comcast would use, to the customer. Xfinity/Comcast uses this private network when there is no internet present, allowing service workers access when they cannot establish a connection to a modem. In essence, this serves as another way for the We.piranha to sneak into your home, and private internet, through your provider.

3. Backbone—Very similar to the backhaul, the Backbone is described as the core infrastructure of a network. It provides high-speed connectivity and serves as the main conduit for data traffic. The various hardware you use, such as routers, switches, and so forth—are the main components of the Backbone. Unfortunately, one of these main components, albeit unwanted, could also be the We.piranha. It is said one can gain access to the Xfinity/Comcast Backbone by using the wireless Backhaul GRE. This can be achieved by using a modem belonging to someone else, such as a neighbor, for connection to the Backbone.

4. Presidential/Secret Service device—This device is a defense tool utilized by the United States Secret Service to protect the president and other high-profile individuals. This device is a United States defense device. Labeled primarily for its anti-drone features, it is engineered to disable or neutralize any drone or flying object if it comes too close to the president. Whilst intended as a protective measure, this device has been abused and misused by trolls and hackers, making it a weaponized national security threat.

5. Tactical device made by Pegasus Intelligence—Known as PTWIS, or Pegasus Tactical WiFi Interception Sensor. Pegasus states the device is a piece of technology designed for military and security applications. The primary function is to monitor and intercept wireless communications over Wi-Fi networks. Furthermore, it is typically used by law enforcement, military, and intelligence agencies for surveillance and network security purposes.

6. Israeli Wi-Fi Interception Kit—The Israeli firm selling this device boasts it can be operated remotely and can connect an attacker to as many as 50 targeted devices at once. Israelis also emphasize their piranha enables both surveillance and man-in-the-middle attacks; potentially facilitating cyberattacks by trolls/hackers. This version of the piranha is weatherproof and has a battery life/can be programmed for up to four days.

7. The Ukrainian Piranha AVD 360–Developed by the Ukrainian company Piranha-Tech, the Piranha AVD 360 is an electronic warfare(EW) system designed to protect military forces from drone threats. Ukraine highlights their piranha has a very powerful arsenal at hand. The system jams the signal, which drones use, to communicate and receive commands. This can cause drones to fall out of the sky, hang in the air, or make an emergency landing.

In addition to the above, the Ukrainians assert their version of the piranha has significant defensive features. The Piranha AVD 360 creates a protective dome around itself. The system also prevents drones from transmitting data and receiving commands. Furthermore, it has the capability to jam satellite navigation systems, enhancing its effectiveness against drone threats.

One might assume all these different versions of the piranha, marketed by all of these different entities, are making the Wi-Fi interception industry more competitive than ever—on the contrary—they all represent the same underlying piranha technology.

Each version of the piranha device boasts it can perform various similar tasks, but deep down inside they all bleed the same color, piranha!

One way to think of it is similar to a piranha device cloned in a lab. A direct copy of the piranha could be made and sent anywhere around the world. The person receiving it could paint it, add an extra part, or whatever else, but all modifications aside—it is still the exact same lab-created piranha.

Findings also indicate all these versions of the piranha were allegedly developed to counter outside threats, but self-preservation is another significant commonality these piranhas' possess. The piranha—including the We.piranha—will evolve and adapt to any situation, whether offensive or defensive. For this reason alone, we must be smart and tactful, fighting back against the piranha.

On paper, this encompasses most of the essentials the We.piranha has to offer; in reality, it can do much more. This will be examined as we progress. Throughout various stages of the book, we will also continue a deeper dive into the proficiencies of the piranha.

It is unclear which came first, the chicken or the egg, meaning which version of the piranha came first. Honestly, does it matter? No, probably not! Since becoming relevant, all of these devices have been hacked, stolen, and misused in ways not originally intended. Because of this, the We.piranha has become more of a hush-hush topic.

We have placed the stones down for the foundation and established it does not matter which version of the piranha is attacking you. What does matter is to cleanse. We must wash the piranha away, from our lives, as soon as possible.

Therefore, knowing the distance the We.piranha can travel is very crucial. Data suggests the We.piranha has a radius of approximately 2100 feet. With extenders and other accessories, one would be wise to assume the piranha can go much, much farther. Take note, the piranha has the capability to geolocate devices, but only within the stated capable radius. By this, I mean once the hacker knows certain information about the target, the hacker can go outside of the We.piranha radius—to anywhere in the world—and still target the specific device it initially intended to attack.

Knowing the capable distance of the We.piranha helps define how far away your troll/hacker is located. This will provide us a nostalgic point of view, detailing whom is trolling us.

—Chapter 3—

Next, we delve into the identity of the troll/hacker controlling the piranha. Oftentimes, more than one troll/hacker is committing the We.piranha crimes. For the most part, we will assume we are only battling one, at large, troll/hacker; but some references might include more than one person.

Thus, we must identify the person targeting you. If we know whom is manipulating the We.piranha, it will be much easier to resolve the issue.

Start by using the 5W's and H method. Commonly used in journalism, this approach is often taught, in school, as we grow up—whom, what, when, where, why, and how.

These helpful journalism guidelines may not answer all your questions; however, they will be very useful in gathering essential information about your specific situation and events.

1. Whom?

Whom is targeting you? Look within the radius—target area—of the We.piranha. This is where you are most likely to find your culprit. Think of it as an inner circle. Start with the closest neighbor and work outward. When dealing with the We.piranha, it is unfortunate, but you must look at the negative in the people closest to your house and proximity. Most of the time, the nicest, most social, friendliest, and unassuming people are the individuals sending the piranha attacks.

2. What?

What could be the possible reason or intention of each one of these suspects? Some possibilities include financial gain, possible hatred toward you, any type of military affiliation, or connections to your family and friends. There is also the possibility there is no reason. This is the possibility they might simply get a rush, or fetish gratification, out of being a troll/hacker.

What device is the piranha attacking? Is it attacking your cell phone? Is it attacking your computer or tablet? Depending on the devices you own, we must narrow down which of your devices the We.piranha is targeting.

3. When?

When does the piranha attack? Is there a specific time of day when these attacks usually occur? Take detailed notes and look for patterns over several consecutive days as you will want to reference each day. Logging information will help determine if the We.piranha is in auto-attack mode.

Document every detail meticulously—trust the process. You can never have too many notes. Even if something seems irrelevant at the moment, write it down anyway; you will be grateful you did in the long run.

Does the piranha attack when you are watching television? Does it attack when you are surfing the internet on a computer or tablet? These are the types of—when's—you will want to observe closely.

4. Where?

Where is the piranha attacking you? Is it attacking a particular side of your house or property? Is the attack occurring in a specific location inside your computer (e.g., services, control panel, media and features, etc.)?

Most likely, the answer to all these questions is yes. Not to mention your cell phone. Is it attacking your cell phone? If so, it is crucial to identify exactly where inside your cell phone the piranha is attacking.

Remember to consider your Virtual Private Network(VPN); the We.piranha often targets and exploits vulnerabilities in VPNs. Do your best to narrow down all these locations.

5. Why?

Why is the piranha attacking you, your devices, your home, and your property? The most common motivation is always going to be financial gain and/or personal vendetta, but there are other reasons as well.

Location can also be a significant consideration. If you live near the person controlling the We.piranha, you may become a target due to your proximity.

Think of every possibility and do not rule anything out!

6. How?

How is the We.piranha attacking you? Is it attacking you through the internet or the Ethernet? Keep in mind these are two separate things—they are not the same. There are other ways in, too. Watch for Raspberry phone internet connections, hotspots, Bluetooth, Ethernet over Power, Power over Ethernet, Loopback Interfaces, Backbone, Backhaul, and Intranet connections. These are the various types of connections I have personally witnessed coming and going from my computers and devices, courtesy of the We.piranha.

I understand what you might be thinking right now—none of these connections seem very logical! Well, speaking abruptly, you are not crazy! Nothing with the piranha is logical. Somehow, in some way, they all create their own unique connection. The purpose is to allow the piranha access to your personal information and devices. This is theft at a very sophisticated level. We will address this more in-depth, later on, when we discuss computers and tablets.

If certain statements sound repetitive, I apologize, but they must be drilled into your mind. Do not forget I am your ally, and if there is one person whom believes you and the things happening to you, it is me.

As such being said, be very diligent and open-minded, as you will want to look everywhere for clues. The We.piranha does not discriminate; it will attack anything and everything. Remember, when used the wrong way, the piranha is an ever-evolving, eternally evil device.

Getting back to possible suspects...

The most likely candidate will be one of your closest neighbors. This means the perpetrator is someone you most likely know and interact with on a daily basis. Open your internet connections, on one of your devices, and look at the networks surrounding you. You may use this as a starting point to identify the troll/hacker.

You should see the We.piranha in the list as a very strong signal, probably coming from your own house. Keep an eye on the other networks, too; they are all clues. More than likely, your perpetrator has numerous internet connections, hence every connection on the list is important. Subsequently, at least one of these internet connections probably goes back to your perpetrator, thus think carefully about these connections.

If you still cannot narrow down the identity of your troll/hacker, do not worry. We will use more tools and tactics to discover the identity of this person or persons as we progress. To put the proximity in perspective, the couple right next door to me, to the west, are my perpetrators.

Try to get in the mindset of how you would think and react if you were the troll/hacker. If we understand the mind of the person—or people—behind the piranha, then we can better understand the piranha itself.

Do not rule out a spouse or roommate as an accomplice; it is very likely a team effort. In my case, the male neighbor, to the west, is more of the—action—troll. He hangs cameras, installs, lights, sets up switches, strings extension cords, etc. whilst his wife operates more behind the scenes.

The hacking is a mutual effort, but for the most part, the wife stays hidden because she does not like the confrontation. Preparedness and doing your homework are key to fighting the piranha—there is probably more than one puppet master pulling on the piranha strings here.

No matter what the answers are to the questions mentioned earlier in this chapter, there is one thing for certain, never underestimate the We.piranha. If we underestimate the piranha, it will take advantage of us. It takes advantage of everything. It lies, cheats, and steals.

For this matter, we must be on the lookout for chicanery or trickery. Do not be surprised if you encounter unwanted piranha games!

—Chapter 4—

The puppet master pulling the puppet strings of the piranha attacking me calls themself a White Witch. This alleged White Witchcraft is a common term when discussing the person controlling the piranha.

If we dive into the whole White Witch concept, this villainous, pagan sorcery brings much trickery.

White Witchcraft is a form of magic intended to be used for good—such as healing or protection. White Witches are also said to follow ethical rules and avoid harming others.

On the other hand, Black Witchcraft is a form of magic intended to be used for harm—such as to control or harm enemies. As we can see when dealing with White and Black Witches, the opposite is true here as the troll/hacker controlling the piranha exhibits the typical signs of trickery. If witches are real and my troll/hacker is a witch, they sure as hell are not a White Witch, but rather a Black Witch! They call themself one thing, but they are really another. They say they are good, but they are really bad. They say they are a cat, but they are really a dog—per se. The metaphors go on and on, but the one consistency here is the trickery.

I cannot say I believe in witches—again, per se—but I can say I do believe in the strength and trickery of the piranha. The troll/hacker controlling the piranha is always trying to convince the victim about false statements. This leads us to Rogry. The perpetrator whom will not leave me alone, always says this is the time for Rogry or, more abruptly, the We.piranha controls Rogry.

The irony here, Rogry is defined as—deplorable behavior!

I know! Go figure! I believe the whole Witchcraft stuff is a bunch of—hocus pocus—but the lies and deceit are very real.

THE WE.PIRANHA

Whilst White Witchcraft and Rogry might seem a little offbeat, we must understand the mastermind behind the piranha to understand the piranha. The whole concept is extremely strange, but it is very real to them so we must take it seriously. This is why we discuss this very unique topic and others.

The more strange and unreal things might seem, reality is the opposite. These types of things, and things similar to them, are reality in the world of the We.piranha.

At this point, I am going to paint a picture in your mind—a picture of how trolls/hackers behind the We.piranha manipulate and trick us using this very powerful device we have come to know as the We.piranha.

I do not have viable solutions for most of these tricks, as I am merely presenting them to you to be aware of them.

In no distinct order...

—Trick 1—

Keep an eye out for multiple fake USB/drives on your computer. These are virtual drives placed there by the We.piranha. Essentially, if you have a USB drive plugged into your E and/or F drive, you may also see fake drives appear in your G, H, etc. This is not a computer glitch; rather, intentionally placed there by the piranha.

Fake virtual drives are very common for the piranha. They are used to steal your personal information. On your end of the computer, they are fake, over where the piranha is located, they are real virtual USB drives. Whilst you are researching and storing information on your real drive, the fake virtual drives are downloading and stealing everything—new information, old information, everything is at risk of being stolen.

—Trick 2—

Watch for fake virtual routers and modems. The We.piranha has the capability of replacing your real modems and routers with an identical virtual copy, rendering your devices obsolete. This happened to me.

My router was replaced with an identical virtual copy, making it impossible for me to use my real router. I discovered this when I saw my router listed amongst the Wi-Fi networks, even though it was not plugged in nor booted up. One day, after my router had been unplugged and disconnected for over one week, I attempted to log into my Wi-Fi network.

I typed in my password, and other login information, but it indicated my router was already in use. This prompted me to investigate the strange circumstances. An identical copy mimicking my router was showing up as already in use!

—Trick 3—

My troll/hacker, using the We.piranha, loves to perform man-in-the-middle attacks. The one used most often against me and my devices is the—evil twin—attack.

Evil twin attacks are a type of man-in-the-middle(MITM) attack, but not the same thing. An evil twin attack specifically involves a fake Wi-Fi network appearing to be legitimate, whereas MITM attacks encompass any scenario where an attacker intercepts communication between two parties.

The purpose of these attacks is always malicious. Sometimes they are aimed at stealing data, engaging in phishing, hacking, making unauthorized purchases, etc.; other times, the intention is simply to be a computer troll.

The evil twin attack creates what is known as an—evil twin—turning the real router down by attacking and rerouting traffic to this new, but fake, access point. As a result, the victim inadvertently connects to the evil twin. This makes the original router encryption data irrelevant.

I think it is safe to say anyone dealing with the piranha is probably facing man-in-the-middle attacks, specifically the evil twin attack. We know this because, well, it is the piranha and the attacker is a troll.

There are several signs for you, as the victim, to watch for if you suspect a man-in-the-middle attack. These signs include frequent unexpected disconnections, seeing unfamiliar URLs on websites you normally use, experiencing slower internet speeds, encountering unexpected pop-ups asking for login details, noticing missing HTTPS in the address bar, or connecting to public unsecured Wi-Fi networks without proper precautions. Essentially, any situation where your online activity seems unusual or where you are prompted to provide sensitive information on a suspicious-looking website could indicate a man-in-the-middle attack.

Keep an eye out for these attacks, as they can be very frustrating and annoying. To date, I have yet to find a complete solution to these attacks.

—Trick 4—

The We.piranha has the capability of mimicking MAC addresses and even creating brand-new, real MAC addresses. This is different from spoofing, as the piranha is generating genuine MAC addresses. Spoofing is defined as disguising oneself as a trusted source to gain access to personal information or steal money.

Does the piranha spoof? Absolutely, but it also creates real, genuine MAC addresses. Keep in mind a MAC address is, a unique identifier, hardcoded into each device by the manufacturer. This means a new one cannot be generated and recognized as legitimate on a network without physically altering the hardware itself.

Subsequently, the lesson here—it is nearly impossible to create a new, real MAC address. Nevertheless, we all know the piranha defies all odds and makes the impossible, possible! The piranha can create several nearly identical MAC addresses in sequence, likely with only one letter or number different—most often at the end of the address, but these are not real Mac addresses. The odds of acquiring several devices with MAC addresses in sequence are extremely low. You would be more likely to see a piranha(fish) drinking a Mai Tai on a beach in Mexico. Then again, you never know whilst scrapping with the We.piranha; it has been pouring telemetry down my throat for over five years now!

There are ways to figure out these real, but fake, MAC addresses. There's a little-known ace up your sleeve which can be used to discover these MACs. I am talking about deauthers, which we will discuss in depth a little later. Whilst there are other ways to find out the MAC addresses, the deauther route is the path I chose.

In my experience, one common occurrence with this trick is the We.piranha will change one number, or letter, in the Mac address. This is, of course, hoping you will not notice. As stated above, it is usually a very small similar occurrence, making them strikingly hard to detect. For example, the piranha will change an—A—to a—4—or a—B—to a—6. Think very subtle when looking for this conniving piranha tactic.

—Trick 5—

The We.piranha will attach fake virtual drives and other devices to your router. You can discover this by going to your router homepage. As soon as you log in, visually inspect the external devices/drives section. You must be quick, as the piranha is very quick too.

Look for the—externals—area, specifically where it shows the number of devices attached to your router. It will probably jump from 1 or 2 over 1 or 2(1/1 or 2/2) to 0/0. This change occurs very rapidly because, as soon as you log in, the trickery begins. The piranha changes the display from stating 1/1 device(s) to 0/0 device(s) attached. This is a way of making you believe nothing is there—hence the We.piranha trickery. Therefore, watch very closely as this will be extremely quick!

—Trick 6—

The piranha will lie to you regarding the devices allegedly connected to your internet. Under your router's homepage, glance at the—devices connected—section. Every device you see will probably be an alleged exact, identical copy of your device. Realistically speaking, what you are witnessing is probably not true. Devices appearing online may not actually be yours, and you might find yourself questioning how specific devices are online when you know for a fact they are completely shut off and offline.

My advice is to kick all the devices, essentially forcing a sweep of everything connected to your internet. More than likely, the fake devices will return, but at least you have the satisfaction of annoying the troll/hacker behind the piranha attacks.

—Trick 7—

This is a cause-and-effect trick. The cause is you touch the piranha. The effect is you get zapped. The solution is do not touch the piranha.

Let me explain...

If the We.piranha does not like something you are doing, it will—zap you! This is not a physical zap, this is a virtual zap! This means it will freeze whatever you are doing on your device. This freeze can last upward of 90 seconds. Whether surfing the internet, trying to get online, changing settings, etc. it will—zap you!

Again, to reiterate, if you feel or experience a freeze in your device, even if you just sense it emotionally—you have just been zapped by the piranha!

—Trick 8—

Falling in line with zapping, be vigilant for imitated internet connections. If your internet connection is called Network ABC, the piranha may create a second, duplicate network also named Network ABC. This occurs quite often! If you attempt to connect to the wrong Network ABC, the piranha will zap you, again.

To avoid this situation, if you notice a second duplicate Network ABC, double-check the IP and MAC address associated with the network. This will help identify the legitimate Network ABC.

—Trick 9—

When logging onto your internet connection, be alert for subtle differences in how you are prompted to log in. Variations within the login process are a common ploy. For instance, you might wonder why your network is asking for a password when it already knows the password. This is trickery!

If you provide your password in such a situation, it is sent back to the piranha, leading to the theft of more personal information and causing further damage. This is cause-and-effect, therefore, if your network is requesting a password when you believe it should not be, or when it already knows the password, do not enter it. Instead, back out or cancel when prompted.

Depending on the device you are using, you will learn ways to navigate around these types of scams. Stay vigilant for similar tricks related to passwords and other sensitive information in various contexts. Lesson learned—we must—learn the ways of the piranha!

—Trick 10—

In this discussion, we turn the attention to cell phones and tablets, where I have observed this irritating piranha tactic most frequently. The We.piranha has the ability to alter battery life of these devices, causing the life cycle to fluctuate unpredictably. You may notice rapid increases or decreases in battery performance which remain inconsistent, and plugging in or unplugging the device does not appear to remedy the issue. The piranha just plays the game it wants to play.

The crucial aspect, watch for quick spikes and quick declines in the battery life of your devices. Moving in similar waters, the piranha also enjoys altering metadata. An easy way to watch for metadata changes is through date and time on your device. The random alteration of date and time on your device, seemingly with no reason at all, will leave you puzzled. In most cases, there is nothing wrong with your device. This is just the piranha, once again, being the piranha.

You can try simple remedies such as restarting your device, but we are far too savvy to the games the We.piranha plays. Sometimes, if a plausible solution eludes us, the best course of action may be to simply ignore the annoyance.

—Trick 11—

If you ever wonder how the piranha always breaches your firewall and antivirus undetected, this is a likely candidate. Operating under the guise of military deceit, the We.piranha convinces your devices and network it deserves access. This is because it masquerades as Xfinity/Comcast.

Consider this—the master device for Xfinity/Comcast is likely to be granted access to your network, or any network for that matter. At this point, the We.piranha would not be classified as malware, spyware, or spam. As the master device, your equipment believes the piranha is supposed to be there.

Once you grasp this concept, it all falls into place and makes sense. It is actually quite clever. Your network has been outfoxed by the fox—or, in this case, out-piranha-ed by the piranha!

—Trick 12—

Speaking of having a fox—or a piranha—in your henhouse, it is important to note the piranha enjoys playing around within VPNs. It can make you, and your device, believe you are not connected to your network when, in reality, you are still connected.

Be especially cautious of double VPNs. The piranha has been known to initiate multiple VPNs, simultaneously, which causes your device to disconnect from the internet, but yet still show internet status as connected.

Stay vigilant in this scenario. Even if your device indicates it is connected to the internet, question the status. What you are probably witnessing is a deceptive facade; in reality, you are not connected to the internet. Possible solutions for these VPN issues will be addressed later in the method section.

—Trick 13—

The We.piranha is skilled at making you believe your device(s) are defective when, in fact, they are perfectly fine. I refer to this tactic as—faulty to factory. The piranha manipulates you into thinking your device is malfunctioning, pressuring you to restore factory settings.

This allows the evidence of the We.piranha to be erased from your device(s) allowing the piranha to start the cycle all over again. This type of trickery is most commonly performed on computers.

—Trick 14—

Diving into computers a little bit, the tricks are never-ending. The cunning We.piranha can unleash malware, spyware, and spam; often undetectable to most antivirus and firewalls. It plants malware in the computer, making the operating system believe it is—not genuine. This is another force-play for faulty to factory.

The piranha can conceal itself within your firewall, antivirus software, and various applications, making it a master of disguise. It lurks everywhere, and it is crucial to be aware of the signs; the tricks are pervasive within your computer.

In many ways, this serves as a testament to the troll lurking behind the We.piranha. Whilst the troll remains hidden, the piranha flinches as a frightened little —bellyfish. Ironically, just like everything else in this scenario, the piranha is ultimately —belly up—in deceit when it comes to computers.

—Trick 15—

Getting kicked off the internet is never fun; the We.piranha has the capability to do just this. The piranha can deauthorize, jam, or otherwise disrupt any device the hacker commands it to attack. This can go on for minutes, hours, days, basically as long as the troll/hacker wants it to occur.

Using a tablet as an example, it can boot the tablet off the internet, forcing you to reboot, resign into the internet, and more. The We.piranha can even use this trick to affect an entire household all at once. Sometimes restarting the modem and/or router solves this issue, but often times it does not.

The piranha does not stop at just internet connected devices; it can do this same trick to stoves, water heaters, furnaces, and anything else with a computer chip. At times, the only option is to wait until the troll has had enough trolling and allows us to regain access.

One bright note about this trick; all evidence suggests it is not in the troll/hacker(s) best interest to maintain it indefinitely. As much fun as it may be for him to attack in this manner, it appears he suffers some consequences for performing this trick over long periods. Maybe it ties up too many piranha resources and he needs it for other malicious activities. Worst-case scenario, we simply ride it out until we are set free and allowed to use our own equipment—again!

—Trick 16—

This brings us full circle to the heartbeat of the piranha! I categorize glitches as the final trick in the We.piranha's arsenal of evil doings. Whilst we have touched on a few glitches, countless others remain undiscovered and unacknowledged. Whenever you encounter a glitch, there is a strong chance it is the piranha at work.

Do not rule out any glitches when scrapping with the We.piranha; this is the most devious trick of them all. Regardless of the magnitude, device, network, or situation, nothing can be ruled out. Many of the other tricks are extremely crucial, but the piranha's ability to spawn glitches is pervasive. Your internet provider, or other utility companies, might try to convince you the issue resides solely in your device. However, if you find yourself dealing with a piranha problem, it is likely what you are experiencing is not merely a glitch.

Remember there are no coincidences when scrapping with the We.piranha. Others might not believe you and might say you are stretching the truth or you are crazy when you talk about the piranha, to say it politely. But I stand by you—I believe you 100%.

The key here, question everything. Do not second-guess yourself, as your instincts are probably spot on from the very beginning. A glitch is not just a glitch! This is Rogry at its finest, and engaging with the We.piranha amounts to a high-stakes evil game of chicken—a sinister game indeed!

There are, of course, other tricks in the piranha's playbook, but these are some of the more common ones I have come across. Keep a watchful eye out as you will probably see other, new, ever-evolving tricks of the trade!

Now we understand a vast amount of the trickery the We.piranha brings to the table. We have also narrowed down and possibly identified the troll/hacker. The next step I suggest is to try to eradicate the We.piranha, from your life, via one of the methods listed below.

Based on my research and experience with the We.piranha, I have listed several methods, in no specific order, to help solve or mitigate your piranha issue. Whilst each of these methods has a chance to remedy your piranha problems, there is an equal chance they will not; hence, be prepared.

—Chapter 5—

We cannot be pros at kicking piranha ass unless we are actively fighting it. We will start the method section becoming proactive with our credentials!

—Method 1—

—Change Usernames, Passwords, Emails and all Login Information—

Right from the get-go I will tell you I do not believe this method is very effective. In my experience, changing any of my personal information, such as username, password, email, or any other login information, has resolved absolutely nothing.

Although I do not believe this is a very effective resolution, whilst fighting the We.piranha, I am hopeful it might help someone. If you are going to try this path, keep in mind just about every device you own has an area where one can type in verification credentials.

As soon as you believe you have typed in new credentials on all your devices, take a step back and double-check your list. Everything must be safeguarded. There are probably more devices and more credentials with adjustable settings. Remember to check all phones, tablets, computers, televisions, DVD players, and, probably most importantly, modems and routers. Make sure every device—and I mean every—has been checked and double-checked. Do not forget about any hotspots or access points you might have.

Additionally, ensure you check any devices your children or other family members have, as these credentials will need to be changed too. Look in areas of your device where it connects to your network, but there could be other, lesser-known, locations depending on the device. Disconnect and then reconnect every device you have, as this will give them all a fresh start.

This method is fairly straightforward. When I was attempting this method, I found myself going back, several days later, and realizing there was another device—and another device—I forgot to check. The important aspect is to be diligent and thorough. The piranha will seek out any device left untouched.

The speed, of which, you type in your password, and keeping it hidden, does not seem to matter here—or at least it did not in my case. Hence the piranha's ability to perform a—workaround!

For these reasons, I do not believe this method is very effective. The piranha learns to evolve and adapt, and works around anything and everything.

—Method 2—

—Complain to Xfinity/Comcast—

Whether or not you currently have services from Xfinity/Comcast is not relevant. What is relevant is the We.piranha coming into your house, devices, and life is backed by Xfinity/Comcast, making it their problem as well as yours.

Over the years, I have dealt with hundreds of various Xfinity/Comcast workers in my quest to eradicate the piranha. To date, nothing I have said nor done has made any difference with these workers. However, I do have some logics you can graze over with them.

First of all, if you are going to get anywhere with these people, you will have to speak to corporate and/or someone in high authority. Do not waste your time with online or over-the-phone chat.

Xfinity/Comcast also has what they call a CSA team. This stands for Customer Security Assurance and is a service which allegedly helps customers report online safety issues. The CSA team can potentially assist with spam and phishing emails, firewall attacks, identity theft, blocked websites, and more. However, in my experience, the CSA team is just another group of workers with a fancy name.

Be prepared for all these workers to play dumb, naïve, and coy. Do not fall for this; any Xfinity/Comcast employee with even a modicum of competence should know what the We.piranha is, and if they do not, they should be fired(my opinion only).

Obviously, the first thought, tell them whatever you can to get them to help you. This would include telling them their master installation device is causing extreme interference with your personal Wi-Fi signal in your house. You might also mention the signal is stuck in your system and there are no Xfinity/Comcast workers in the area, so it should not be there.

Make them understand the signal is inside your house, because 100%, no doubt, the We.piranha is inside your house. If they play dumb or coy about the We.piranha, tell them the Backhaul GRE is causing interference and you need the signal removed. Alternatively, you can mention the Backbone to the internet is causing too much interference and you need them to address it.

Finally, try asking them to move your cable line to the other side of the power pole, or even better, to a completely new pole altogether.

These are some of the best pitches you can try and present to the Xfinity/Comcast workers. Otherwise, you must argue, argue, argue with them.

On the flipside, be prepared for the workers to try and sell you a new modem and/or router. Do not fall for this one; remind them the Piranha Gateway, as they like to call it, is not yours.

They might try to tell you they can install a MoCA(Multimedia Over Coax Alliance) interference prevention filter on your main cable line, but this will not work. The MoCA filter actually slowed down my internet, all the while, helping my troll become a more powerful troll.

The MoCA filter is intended to prevent interference between MoCA signals and other devices in your home. However, in my case, it only prevented outside interference for the piranha, essentially blocking everything else but the Piranha. The MoCA filter assists the Backhaul GRE and makes the We.piranha behave as if it were hopped up on steroids. It felt as if a virtual fish jumped out of the water and smacked me in the face with its pumped-up tail fin!

Of course, the We.piranha was still there inside my house. This slimy little virtual creature made me feel like I was the fish out of water. As quick as the Xfinity/Comcast worker installed the MoCA filter, I uninstalled it even quicker and threw it in the garbage. The MoCA filter specializes in mass data transfer; similarly, it helps the We.piranha specialize in identity theft! For this reason alone, the MoCA filter must go in the garbage!

Moving along, more than likely none of these Xfinity/Comcast employees will be able to help you. However, you are welcome to try and speak with any, and every, one of these people and/or groups of people you wish. This will, at the very least, document it for you. Lastly, ensure Xfinity/Comcast does not try to charge you for any issues. Remember, this situation is not your fault.

—Method 3—

—Complain to Local Police Department—

If the Xfinity/Comcast route does not work, try this path.

This solution is a double-edged sword. When I went this route, the police said, in a nutshell, you have nothing tangible and there is nothing there. I cannot even count how many times I have heard the police say, nothing tangible and nothing there. Unfortunately, When the troll/hacker found out I went to the police, it gave him a sick, twisted form of arousal.

The troll/hacker controlling the Piranha attacking me received a phone call from the local police department. The police asked my troll and his wife, AKA troll two, to stop the attacks via the We.piranha. Naturally, my troll/hacker did not comply, and the situation only worsened.

There is a chance your experience would end different for you, but this is the way it ended for me.

Before escalating matters to this level, ensure you have gathered as much evidence as possible to present to the police. Having comprehensive documentation will strengthen your case and help them understand the situation better.

You will likely start off discussing your situation with low-ranking beat cops. Do not be discouraged; this is actually a positive step. The higher up the chain this goes, with the police department, the less they are willing to help. Many of the beat cops genuinely want to help, but they do not have the power, authority, or resources to take significant action.

In contrast, higher-ranking officers, such as sergeants and detectives, may be more dismissive. They often turn a blind eye, struggle to believe the severity of your situation, or simply view it as a waste of their time.

As mentioned earlier, gathering evidence is crucial. Whilst photographs can be valuable, they may be challenging to acquire. One key image you should aim to capture is a screenshot of the We.piranha connection listed amongst the available internet connections.

Take note of the connections immediately surrounding the We.piranha network. The same person whom owns one, and possibly more, of these connections is likely your perpetrator. If you believe you know the identity of this person, then start looking at them as a suspect. Gather additional evidence to support your suspicions.

Next, get a network analyzer application/program. Wireshark is a great option, and it is free. If you decide to use Wireshark you can only use it on a PC, but this is my recommendation and in my opinion, the best option.

Wireshark allows you to analyze protocols whilst capturing and monitoring traffic entering and leaving your network in real-time. This allows you to troubleshoot network issues, investigate security vulnerabilities, and understand how applications communicate across your network by examining the details of data packets at a low level. In essence, Wireshark helps you—see—what is happening on your network by dissecting individual packets of data.

If you are not very computer-savvy and knowledgeable, about this type of stuff, it might be difficult at first. Once you learn to use Wireshark, this will be a valuable tool in your search for a positive resolution.

I have personally noticed when I am being attacked by the We.piranha, there is a massive amount of—mass data transfer—coming and going from my network. Subsequently, when dealing with the We.piranha, it is very important to have a strong and efficient network analyzer, such as Wireshark.

More than likely, you will be looking for Wireshark entries with names such as Cadant, Technicolor(USA), Vantiva USA, CommScope, Asustek, Arista Network, and Azure. Take all MAC addresses you find under these entries and run them through a reverse MAC address lookup website. Each of these entries will be related to the We.piranha. Any entry appearing under Cadant, Technicolor(USA), CommScope, or Vantiva USA is 100% the We.piranha.

Keep an eye out for a very elusive entry known as Cantina Thompson's US Subsidiary, as this is also associated with the piranha. You may encounter other connections in your journey, but these are the ones I have come across. Be very thorough in your research whilst using Wireshark.

There may also be entries mimicking your own devices, so be cautious. The We.piranha has the capability to hide and appear as if it were one of your devices. For example, if you see an entry giving the impression it is your television, including the brand, but it appears out of place—investigate it thoroughly.

When using Wireshark, note the times of all suspicious entries. Correlate these times to when your potential suspect is coming or going from their house. Also, note when your device shows as online. Should your device be online at this point? These entries are very likely piranha entries—triggered manually by the perpetrator.

If you see an entry resembling your TV or any other device and you find it suspicious, try narrowing it down by unplugging the television or device. Once unplugged, monitor for any further entries of such nature over the course of several hours, especially when your suspect is coming or going. Make sure you unplug it. This is very important. You cannot turn the TV/device off. You must unplug it, as the piranha will continue to abuse and misuse the TV/device.

If you simply turn the TV or device off but leave it plugged in, it is likely still actively being hacked; hence you would continue to see entries for it in Wireshark.

Getting back to photos, the more you have when approaching local law enforcement, the better. Take pictures of everything, even if you are unsure if it is related to your case, take pictures.

You can take pictures of evidence you come across on social media platforms; however, my local police department indicated they needed more for them to help me. More than social media posts, more evidence, and more specifically, more tangible evidence. I hope your local police department is more cooperative and open-minded than mine was for me.

Make a list of important websites, such as websites about the Israeli version, Pegasus, etc. These may or may not be useful, but you will definitely want them for your reference and in your arsenal.

Use your personal knowledge and experiences you have dealt with during this whole ordeal as evidence as well. Personal experiences are usually thought of by local police departments as a powerful tool. This is another form of evidence, and this is your testimony.

Remember anything you have personally witnessed, tasted, heard, smelled, or touched is your personal knowledge and experiences. These sensory details are the building blocks for your testimony.

Video evidence is a valuable tool in your arsenal. Gather as much video evidence as you can, as this could and should be crucial to your local police department. We will discuss video evidence more fine-tuned in the method following this one.

In my experience, the police will not help you—at least not me. They view the piranha as a—mythical creature—such as Bigfoot or a Unicorn. On the contrary, I assure you this is no Bigfoot, no Unicorn, and definitely not a mythical creature.

Try to make the police understand you are not out looking for the We.piranha and you do not want to be in this situation. Emphasize if you had it your way, the piranha would be gone! It would be out of your life forever!

—Method 4—

—Video Evidence—

If you do not have a surveillance system protecting your home and property, you will need to invest in one. The initial thought might be to opt for the most expensive, high-tech system available. However, based on my experience, I can tell you this is not the best approach when scrapping with the piranha.

We briefly touched base on the complexity of your setup at the start of this book, and this is where it really comes into play. The We.piranha loves to ruin expensive, high-tech, new-age devices; thus it benefits you greatly to avoid a complex setup. A more advanced surveillance system might work for a while—perhaps a week—until your perpetrator and the We.piranha evolve.

Do not underestimate the piranha; it will evolve, and it does evolve. This is why I always say the piranha is ever-evolving and lurks everywhere around your home, and your property.

We have now established some basics of the video evidence method, therefore I am going to give you some examples of what I have tried and what has worked best for me.

I have a medium-grade wireless surveillance system, but it has not functioned for several months because it is constantly under attack by the We.piranha. This system operated on its own hub, creating a separate network piggybacking off my main network. Before the We.piranha started attacking my system, it worked in optimal condition and was nearly brand new. Once the We.piranha started taking—nibbles—out of it, strange occurrences began. I experienced glitches, half-screen blackouts, green screens, freezing, and disappearing video feeds. The We.piranha also prevented me from downloading and saving my video clips. Alternatively, the piranha would download and save my video clips for the troll/hacker. If my clips were saved to the cloud, the piranha would infiltrate the cloud and compromise the video save settings.

Be vigilant for similar behaviors in your own situation. To combat the We.piranha in this video evidence method, the best approach is to choose the right surveillance system. A wired surveillance system will always be more efficient than a Wi-Fi connected one. Regardless of your choice, opt for a system with the fewest options possible; this reduces the chances of distortion, theft, or erasure of your video evidence by the We.piranha.

In this battle against such a formidable virtual foe, simplicity is key. We fight the fight, but this nasty little virtual fish known as the piranha, hates simplicity!

If we follow the guidelines of—simple is better—there is one surefire way to win whilst trying to gather video evidence. I am talking about trail cameras, but they cannot be just any trail cams. You need to purchase the cameras hunters use when they are out in the wilderness and have absolutely no wireless signal, whatsoever. These trail cameras are commonly known as traditional trail cameras. This is how I won a small feat against the troll/hacker controlling my nemesis, the We.piranha. I switched from Wi-Fi to old-school wired cameras, and I also purchased two traditional trail cameras. If the piranha does happen to hack your trail cams, return them and explain to the workers the cameras are defective. I went through three brands of traditional trail cameras before I found a brand the—puppet master of the piranha—could not hack.

—Method 5—

—Contact Federal Agencies—

Many times talking to your local police department will not solve the piranha problems we face. I do not know why they are so reluctant to help. Maybe they have been compromised or maybe they just do not care. Nevertheless, we do have the option to go above their heads to another agency.

There are several agencies we can turn to for help in accomplishing this goal. I reached out to every agency I could think of to raise awareness about my situation with the We.piranha. Ultimately, it did not work for me, but the more complaints they receive, the more they can no longer ignore the misdeeds of the troll/hacker(s) with a piranha. We must spread the word, and hopefully, at the same time, you will find some resolution.

I did not find a viable way to contact any of them via phone, and civilians do not have the clearance to walk into any of their buildings. This leaves email and filling out forms on the internet.

Some of the more notable agencies I contacted include the FBI, CIA, NSA, Department of Defense, Homeland Security, and multiple cybersecurity agencies. File as many complaints as you can, and remember some of these agencies have more than one location on the internet, to file a claim.

Be prepared to provide a very detailed report regarding the crimes occurring and do not be afraid to file a new complaint every day or every couple of days. This is your right as an American citizen, not to mention your tax dollars pay their salaries. They may not like it, or believe it, but they do work for you!

When I tried this method, I encountered two main issues. First, every one of these departments forwarded my complaints to my local city police department. None of them wanted to deal with me. I guess—out of sight out, of mind—or maybe this was just small fish to them. Either way, once local police received the complaints, they threw them straight in the trash. The city police were angry I went above their heads and expressed how incompetent they were. It did not matter to me if I hurt anyone's feelings! I wanted to be heard, and I wanted the We.piranha gone from my life! I still want these things! Nevertheless, the local police refused to address the issue, so I was back at square one.

Second, once your troll/hacker becomes aware of your current path, he may use the malicious, magical powers of the piranha to block you from all government websites. This happened to me as well. The key is stay adamant and firm in your agenda, continuing to file complaints with one agency after another. Try as many as possible. You can also use different devices; if the troll blocks you from filing on one device, try submitting your complaints from another device. Keep complaining because, remember, you are the victim.

One final thought—assuming you already filed a complaint with your local city police using the earlier method, do not forget to reach out to state troopers or county police as well. Many times, federal agencies will route complaints to state troopers and county police prior to the complaint ever hitting the desk of the city police department. Do not be afraid to use the same evidence with every department you contact.

If this does not work, consider contacting local television stations. Ask if they would be interested in doing a story on the cybercrimes the—troll with the fish—is committing against you.

Be polite, but firm in your endeavors!

—Method 6—

—Faraday Cages, Copper, Tinfoil, other Conduits—

A Faraday cage is defined as a hollow conductive enclosure which shields the contents from electromagnetic radiation and electric charges. The cage works by disrupting and redistributing the charge or radiation around the exterior; effectively canceling it out inside. Simply put, a Faraday cage protects whatever is inside of it, from outside interference. The best materials for constructing a Faraday cage are those which are excellent conductors of electricity. I have listed some common options below.

1. Copper—Excellent conductivity, making it highly effective at blocking electromagnetic fields. It is also relatively easy to work with.

2. Aluminum—Lightweight and corrosion-resistant, aluminum is a popular choice for Faraday cages. It provides great conductivity, though not as high as copper.

3. Steel—Whilst not as conductive as copper or aluminum, steel can still be effective, especially when used in thicker gauges. It is also more durable than other options and can provide structural integrity.

4. Brass—Offers great conductivity, and is resistant to corrosion, though it is less commonly used than copper or aluminum.

My clear choice is aluminum. Copper is too expensive, steel did not work—at all—for me, and I did not try brass. Aluminum seems to be fairly effective, but keep in mind we are fighting the We.piranha. I tried my best with steel, but no matter how I wrapped my devices, the piranha was still able to penetrate the Faraday cage.

This led me to wonder if my internet was being hornswoggled! My internet might be attempting to protect itself from itself. I mean, rhetorically speaking, what if it was trying to protect itself from the master Xfinity/Comcast device?

Obviously, you have to think—outside-the-box—when dealing with the piranha, but I just wondered if the piranha was tricking my internet into believing it was supposed to be there because it was a legitimate Xfinity/Comcast device. Keep in mind I was a customer of Xfinity/Comcast the whole time whilst fighting the We.piranha. For this reason alone, this theory is plausible in my book.

Getting back to conductors, It is time to take a deeper dive into aluminum. The recommended use of aluminum is to wrap each device at least three times, but five times is preferred. I tried wrapping aluminum/tinfoil around my modem, router, and other devices—inside my house—but to no avail! Outside my house—wrapping devices with tinfoil worked well on some, and not so well on others. It did not work wrapping Wi-Fi connected cameras. Alternatively, it seemed to lessen the interference with wired cameras but did not alleviate the problem altogether.

The biggest difference I witnessed was with my traditional trail cameras. This is very important as it pertains to the SD cards. The We.piranha enjoys wiping SD cards clean, causing photos and/or videos to disappear, along with other fishy little tricks.

We can remedy this with tinfoil! Traditional trail cameras, save their content using SD cards. These SD cards are very piranha-friendly which we will now undo.

Wrapping the outer housing of any trail camera, particularly where the SD card is located, is crucial. Tinfoil is, absolutely, one of the best tactics we have for combating the We.piranha. This applies to any security camera using SD cards; however, my experience comes specifically from trail cameras.

Most traditional trail cameras have their lens at the top and the buttons, batteries, power cord, and SD card slot at the bottom. I wrap both the top and bottom with tinfoil, but, obviously, I do not place tinfoil over the lens itself. Instead, I only wrap tinfoil around the outside of the lens area, as the camera must be able to see the world. Honestly, I am not sure if wrapping the top makes a significant difference, but to be safe, I wrap both top and bottom. Depending if I am in a hurry to hide from the troll, I wrap the bottom three to five times. Our purpose here is to protect the SD card. I am not trying to jab a bellyfish with a stick here, but it works. The tinfoil works to protect the SD card. Score one positive point for us victims, and one virtual middle finger for the We.piranha!

Experiment, or play around, with your trail camera settings, as the piranha is extremely finicky about the smallest details. For example, having your trail camera set for 70 feet might make a difference compared to 90 feet. Whilst the piranha might be able to hack the video mode, it may struggle with trail mode or picture mode. Go through the settings and make small changes until you find the best configurations to interrupt and stop the piranha's ability to interfere with your video capture.

Furthermore, make sure you pull the batteries from your trail camera(s) and only use a wired connection. Plug directly into the wall and do not use an extension cord. The SD card slot button needs to be in the up position. I use SanDisk ImageMate Pro SD cards. These are high-quality SD cards and should be widely available. Additionally, I use microSD cards. Bearing in mind, the piranha has the capability to take advantage of the smallest details.

One final thought regarding tinfoil/aluminum. I did try to use tinfoil on my electric meter, the main one—outside my house. I wrapped the entire meter with tinfoil, and the piranha busted through. I told my wife it was as if the piranha was playing some sort of fish out of water trick. It played coy for a while until it flapped and slapped its fin against the side of my meter jolting out an electrical high for the piranha.

The We.piranha employs this same tactic to everything in the target house. It sends out monster surges, or waves, of interference affecting all devices. So the tinfoil on the meter did not work, life moves on, and like always, the piranha kept stealing from me. It really makes you want to commit virtual fishicide, turn the tides and make it the victim's victim.

As I digress, Faraday cages are great when they work. However, we are dealing with the We.piranha. It is important to experiment or play around, with various materials and conduits to see what works best for you. For me, the clear winner is tinfoil.

It works really, really well and is extremely flexible, allowing me to mold it around my devices easily. Not to mention, tinfoil is inexpensive to purchase. We all know fighting the piranha is rarely cheap, so this is a bonus for us all.

—Method 7—

—Spreading the Illusion—

By now, you have probably already complained to Xfinity/Comcast and your local police department. With such being said, it is very likely the troll/hacker is knowledgeable about your knowledge. Assuming your technology and financial situation are inferior to the troll/hacker and the We.piranha, it is time to spread the illusion you are fighting back with firepower of your own. It is time to—troll the troll!

Hackers most commonly fall under one of three different categories. Called—hats—the three main hats of hackers(categories) are white, black, and gray. Other colors of hats round out the rainbow, but these are the three main ones.

—White Hat Hackers—

These are also known as, ethical hackers, these professionals help organizations improve cybersecurity. They identify and fix vulnerabilities in systems.

—Black Hat Hackers—

These hackers exploit system weaknesses to steal, alter, or destroy data. They may also expose data to the public and demand money in return.

—Gray Hat Hackers—

These hackers may break laws or ethical guidelines but do not have malicious intent. They use the internet to find and exploit vulnerabilities in systems.

The hacker behind my We.piranha attack is a black hat hacker as yours most likely is too. To elaborate, black hat hackers are criminals whom break into computer networks with malicious intent. They may also release malware which destroys files, hold computers hostage, steal passwords, credit card numbers, and other personal information. Validation confirmed! Our—piranha troll—is an evil person!

Now we know we are up against a black hat hacker. The most evil type of hacker. A true waste of oxygen and space. Therefore, spreading the illusion via—military deceit—is a go and we are ready!

The idea here is to make the troll/hacker believe we have acquired quite a few new—toys—to fight back! We must make the troll believe we are a—force to be reckoned with!

We can achieve this goal without spending very much money and using our heads. We will use whatever we have lying around as we do not want to spend any more money than we need whilst fighting the We.piranha. You and I, we, are assuming you are being watched like a hawk by your troll, as I am too. To say the least, it is annoying, disgusting, harassing, and an invasion of privacy. We must attempt to thwart this sick, perverted behavior. If we scare him enough, he might stop attacking with the We.piranha. Here we go!

—Example 1—

Fake security cameras can be purchased fairly cheap, at local discount tool stores. I purchased some for under 10 dollars per camera. Search fake security cameras online; they should be available to be purchased locally. If they are unavailable locally, then purchase them online.

An alternative here would be to set up devices around your yard making it appear as if you are watching the troll/hacker(s) every move. Use old cell phones you do not care about, old gaming cameras, etc., basically anything to spread the illusion you are watching them too. Make sure to place your devices in locations the troll/hacker will notice. Also, the devices should be at least six feet away from the property line so you are in compliance with local codes and regulations.

—Example 2—

Build your own fake security camera(s). One idea is to take an old screw or nail box you have lying around and turn it into a camera creation. Start by wrapping the box with tinfoil, or silver heat tape. Next, find something from your house, such as a gem looper, to use as the lens. Finally cut a hole in the box, and shove the looper in the hole. Congratulations! You have now created what appears to be an old-fashioned, disposable Polaroid camera.

As an alternative, you could simply draw a lens in the center of the box. Be creative, and please, for my sake, do not spend very much money. As a matter of fact, I recommend being a cheapskate here.

With our camera now built, it is time to place or hang it. You do not want to hide whilst you hang your new Polaroid camera. I make sure I am visible to my troll/hacker whilst I hang my fake camera(s). The idea is to ensure the troll knows the fake camera is there.

—Example 3—

Get a long wooden stick or a metal rod, but preferably a metal rod. You can buy a metal rod fairly cheap from any local hardware store. I prefer the ones labeled—rebar accessory—in the cement/concrete aisle. There are also metal fence posts, but they tend to be more expensive.

Now you have your metal rod and it is time to go outside, find somewhere close to your troll's house, and pound the metal rod into the ground. Stay at least 6 feet away from the property line to the troll's house. Pound the rod at least 1 foot into the ground, leaving at least 3 feet above ground.

Next, you will want to get yourself a long wire or old extension cord. Run it from the metal rod to somewhere completely obsolete. Just be smart and make sure it appears as if it is wired to your house and doing something important. An example would be to run it under your barbecue, or under the door of your shed. Keep the end running to the house, hidden.

Make the other end of the wire look extremely professional as it connects to the metal rod and winds down toward the Earth. Place a box of some sort at the base of the metal rod and run the wire inside of it. Use a rock, or something else heavy, to place inside the box weighing it down. You can fancy it up with tape or string if you like, but your creation is now complete.

At this point, you are probably asking yourself, what the hell did I just create? My answer is, you are exactly right! You have wire running to a box and a metal rod near the troll's house. Congratulations! It appears as if you have created some sort of homemade hacking device! This will be a mystery to your troll as well. We now hope the troll loses many nights of sleep, pondering this creation sticking out of your yard.

—Example 4—

Take an old Halloween decoration, such as a life-size skeleton, and dress it up. We are going to set him up somewhere you would normally be sitting/standing. This will create the illusion it is you, when it is really not you. I prefer to set the skeleton up behind the blinds on my back porch, but the setting of the skeleton will vary depending on the layout of your house and situation.

Dress him up to make him appear as if he is you. My skeleton does not need pants, as I would only be sitting down on my back porch; thus, he shall be sitting too. I place a hat and T-shirt on him, something heavy on his lap so he does not fall over. And—voila! The bones of the past frighten the bones of the present!

Make sure you move him from time to time. How often, you ask? It does not really matter, as long as he moves. 6 hours, 8 hours, 10 hours—just whenever you get around to it. Think of yourself as a laid-back type of troll fighter! This skeleton trick makes my troll/hacker go schizo, wondering what I am doing on the back porch and why I have been sitting there for hours and hours.

—Example 5—

Go to your local outdoor sporting goods store and purchase a skunk scent bomb. You might have to purchase it online, and it might be called something a little bit different, but we are looking for skunk scent.

My troll hacks from his garage, next to the property line. This creates a perfect opportunity. If a random skunk—happens to pass by—and just—happens to spray—the side of his janky garage, it is not my fault, nor my problem.

I like to get a couple bottles at a time. The first bottle, I always use the whole thing all at once. It is too much fun! I must—no, it is my obligation—to use the whole thing all at once!

I try to make my timing perfect when I believe my troll/hacker will be outside—near his garage. Sometimes my timing is spot on, sometimes it is off. The fresher the scent, the more potent, but it does last for at least three weeks; hence timing is not everything.

If you cannot place your scent bomb near the—hacker hub—be sure to put it somewhere which will annoy him. You could pour it next to their car or dump it on the lawn. You can place it anywhere. Just stay on your own property when you dump it.

Try to be as incognito as possible, but please do not dress up as a big skunk. it could be fun, but I do not believe you will stay hidden this way. Once the troll/hacker notices the smell, and he will, make sure you play extremely coy and savvy. I hope you walk around smiling for the next several days.

When the smell finally dies off, if you purchased more than one scent bomb, you still have at least one bottle left. Use your next bottle at your own discretion.

—Skunk tip—

Re-wetting the original bottle, or affected area of skunk scent, reignites the smell.

There are, of course, many other ways to troll the troll, but these are some of my favorite examples I have used. Place a checkmark, in your mind, next to military deceit and give yourself a pat on the back! The troll has just been trolled!

—Method 8—

—Hide—

This method is fairly straightforward. It is unlikely to work forever, but it might buy you some time.

You must hide. In method 1, we discussed changing usernames, passwords, emails, any and all login information, etc. If you have already tried method 1 and it worked, then great—this time around we will only be changing your network name and password.

Change the name of your WiFi network to an exact duplicate of whichever version of the We.piranha you normally see in your network list(e.g., we.piranha.off, we.piranha.xb6, etc.). If this does not work, you can also try hiding as a duplicate of another nearby network.

—Warning or Caution—

When logging onto your new network name—We.piranha(e.g., .off, .xb6, etc.)—be careful not to log on to the wrong piranha network. If you do happen to attempt to log on to the wrong piranha network, most likely you will get zapped!

—Method 9—

—Revoke the Troll/Hacker(s) Permission—

This method only worked a few weeks for me, but I hope it lasts a very long time for you because it sure is enjoyable.

Jumping right in...There are RF jammers, AKA Wi-Fi jammers, and there are deauthers.

An RF jammer or WiFi jammer broadly disrupts all wireless communication within a certain frequency range by transmitting a strong signal which interferes with other devices' signals. This makes it a more general disruption compared to the targeted approach of a deauther.

A deauther specifically targets and disconnects devices from a particular WiFi network by sending deauthentication frames. Essentially, a deauther is a more precise way to disrupt a specific network, whilst a jammer creates widespread interference across multiple networks.

Another way to look at it...

Wi-Fi jammer—legal to own, illegal to use.

Deauther—legal to own, legal to use in certain circumstances.

Let me explain...

THE WE.PIRANHA

Wi-Fi jammers interfere with authorized radio communications. This goes against the Communications Act of 1934, which prohibits the use of jamming equipment. A Wi-Fi jammer always affects every device in range. This makes them impossible to use in a legal setting, hence legal to own illegal to use.

A deauther is much different than a jammer. A deauther can speak/send protocols which then communicate with a specific, targeted device. Subsequently, they are legal to own and legal to use in a very controlled setting. They can be used when consent has been granted; alternatively, without consent, they are illegal.

Moving forward, we know we have three main players here—the We.piranha, Wi-Fi jammers, and deauthers. We obviously know the piranha is in a league all of its own, and does whatever the hell it wants. We also know we cannot use Wi-Fi jammers, as they will get us in trouble. This brings us to the last one on our list—deauthers.

Deauthers are complicated, sort of a grey area in this game. A grey area we will be using to our advantage. We already know we can legally own a deauther, so how do we use one in a legal manner? We do this by playing—piranha games.

The We.piranha has infiltrated our home and internet. The piranha signal is emitting from within our network. If it wants to act like us, then we must treat it like us! Since we have our own consent, and we know it is not illegal to deauthorize ourselves, we are 100% legal to deauthorize the We.piranha! You heard correct! We have every right to kick this fish out of the water and out of our network.

The Plan...

You will deauthorize the We.piranha. This will kick it off your own internet, and it will be extremely enjoyable in the process. Your troll/hacker will not know what hit him. Deauthorizing the troll brings a lot of pleasure, but if we are going to have fish for dinner, we must first get our hands on a deauther.

Do not spend a lot of money building or purchasing a deauther. If you do, you are getting swindled, and this is the last thing we want to happen. We have all been swindled way too much, for way too long—already—by the piranha.

You could splurge and buy a premade deauther online, but I chose to go the route of building my own. Building a deauther from scratch is fairly inexpensive as long as you have basic computer knowledge, can follow directions, and have enough patience.

—Deauther from Scratch—

Start by purchasing a development board capable of being programmed as a deauther. I used an ESP8266 NodeMCU V2, but feel free to look around at others. The average purchase price of these development boards is 4 to 5 dollars online.

Once you have your board, you will need to search online and figure out how to program it. There are plenty of videos showing how to do this. Closely follow the steps you see in the online videos and you will be fine. You will need to use the computer program Arduino, then download and write the computer code; in turn, you will create your own little deauther—gremlin!

Assuming you have successfully created or purchased a deauther, we will move forward. Following suit with the task at hand, we must perform a few steps before we can attack the piranha.

First, we search the list of Wi-Fi networks your deauther locates. These networks are all within close proximity to you and your house. You should see networks you have never encountered before, as well as some labeled as hidden!

We are close to attacking the We.piranha, but there are still a couple more things to address.

Going back to our video evidence method, use your deauther to gather video evidence. Take pictures of the Wi-Fi networks listed and their Mac addresses. This will come in handy when you go to the police. Even if you do not need a picture of every network listed, we must gather as much potential evidence as possible.

One element to keep in mind, all hidden networks are visible to a deauther and there is absolutely no way to fabricate a MAC address. Deauthers only observe real MAC addresses; they do not observe any fake, spoofed, wannabe, questionable, or any other shady Mac addresses.

Earlier we discussed how unlikely it was to have devices with MAC addresses in sequence. Your deauther may surprise you with what it shows you. Mac addresses in sequence are very common with the piranha. They should not be, but they are. You will see very compelling and damning things; you must take pictures and use them as evidence.

Do not fear showing these pictures from your little deauther gremlin to the police. Remember, it is not illegal to own a deauther, and you cannot deauthorize yourself, so you are fine. You will not get into trouble and can take as many pictures as you wish. The more, the merrier!

It is time to send your deauther gremlin into the den of evil and attack the piranha! Follow the steps given to you online to use your deauther. Once you start the attack, keep your eyes peeled at your suspect's house for anything appearing fishy!

You will not observe any confirmation showing your deauther was successful, but if you did everything correct you will observe confirmation your deauther attack has started. The piranha does have the capability to kick you out of your attack and stop everything you are doing. If this happens, reconnect and start a new attack.

After a few weeks of deauthorizing the We.piranha, my troll/hacker learned to turn the tide on me. He started up his Rogry, hocus pocus shenanigans and began crypto mining my deauther. He also figured out how to use my deauther to deauthorize my devices. Watch for Rogry and any tricks similar to this. If you notice anything suspicious, such as this, stop your attack and wait a few days to start again when the troll does not suspect anything.

One workaround is to erase your development board. This can be achieved by simply reprogramming the code, in turn making the deauther malware-free, clean, fresh, and from scratch. Next, adjust the settings to your liking and restart your attack. Another workaround is to reset your network settings as discussed earlier. You can also try controlling your attacks from a different device or changing the MAC address of your current device. The MAC address of the development board can also be changed through the settings of the deauther homepage.

Additionally, change the MAC address of the deauther's power source(computer) often. Sometimes the troll learns how to use the piranha to reset your deauther back to factory settings himself. Watch for this, as he may want the name of the network to revert to the factory name. You might have to rename the network as quickly as you can before the troll starts trolling you. These small adjustments confuse the We.piranha and allow your attack to proceed.

You might need to use your head and be creative with the deauther. Go through the settings or any other features within the deauther or your device. Use whatever tactic you have to enable your deauther to achieve the attack. Be aware the piranha has the capability to be programmed to manipulate MAC addresses, specific devices, network names, types of attacks, and much more, so be sure to protect your little deauther gremlin.

Finally, whilst using your deauther, pull a page from the piranha's playbook. You and your deauther must be open to ever-evolve in similar fashion to the We.piranha. All these little adjustments matter to the piranha. This is how we fight back, and win, using a deauther.

I will not condone doing anything illegal, but if you believe some of the other networks your deauther observes belong to your troll/hacker, then it is probably time to play piranha games, again(at your discretion)!

—Method 10—

—Turn Bridge Mode Off/Disable—

Bridge mode is a fairly common feature for consumer routers, but not all routers have bridge mode, especially routers with interfaces other than Ethernet.

With this in mind, we will be turning bridge mode off/disabling it; however, on some routers, this could also mean turning bridge mode on/enabling it. Before we proceed with this method, we should ensure we understand the meaning of bridge mode.

Bridge Mode means the router disables all WiFi broadcast and works as a pass-through for the internet to run through to another WiFi router.

Think of Bridge mode as a router disabling its own routing functions. This allows it to act as a simple network bridge or switch. In bridge mode, traffic gets forwarded between different network segments without performing IP address assignment or other routing tasks.

If this sounds familiar, it should—this is right up the piranha's alley. Bridge mode gives the We.piranha the ability to skip certain significant, yet minor, routing tasks. This is why we must turn bridge mode off. If it matters to the piranha, it matters to you!

I cannot provide specifics about turning bridge mode off via your devices, as you will need to check your manufacturer's configuration settings. However, I can say some manufacturers have labeled bridge mode backward, meaning on some devices, turning bridge mode off might actually enable it. Be very careful, do your homework, and choose this setting wisely. You do not want to open the waterway and let the piranha out to swim and play in your network.

We have now learned bridge mode allows multiple routers to connect together. Bridging these routers allows our troll to extend the piranha's reach. This is the last thing the We.piranha needs—more reach!

Some modems have a bridge mode setting, too. This is rare, but not unheard of on a modem. Most often, bridge mode can be found on modem-router combination devices.

We will do the same thing here, with the modem, as we did before with the router— turn off/disable bridge mode. Once you do this, if you have a modem-router combination device, it will disable the router section. Now you will need a separate router to use as a router. Essentially, your modem will solely be a modem.

This unique method to fight the We.piranha has worked for several people, but it has not worked with the troll whom is hacking me. Different modems and/or routers have different settings regarding how to handle this task.

Make sure you check with your specific modem and/or router make and model. Do not forget the goal is to disable bridge mode!

—Method 11—

—Protect the Computer—

—Note—My experience in this section is solely whilst using and protecting Windows operating systems. If you are using a different operating system adjust your defense strategy, and path forward accordingly.

The We.piranha loves to break into computers. To be clear, the piranha cannot swim over to your house and physically break into your computer, thus it does this by virtual means.

—Connection Types—

Any Wi-Fi connection can potentially be breached by the We.piranha. In no particular order, there are various types of connections the piranha is capable of establishing with a computer including internet, Ethernet, Bluetooth, hotspots, Raspberry Pi phone, loopback interface, Backbone, Backhaul GRE, Ethernet over Power, intranet, and probably others as well. These are the connections I have discovered on my computer.

Once the piranha is in a computer, It is nearly impossible to eradicate. The piranha is capable of infiltrating brand new computers straight out of the box, without the computer ever establishing any type of connection. It geolocates the computer and leeches, just like the name insinuates—a piranha.

—Note—I had this happen to me when I purchased a brand-new computer. It took the We.piranha a little less than 12 minutes from the time I booted up my new computer, to the time the piranha was fully embedded in the system. I never established a connection to any network, but the piranha found my computer.

After the piranha leeches to a computer, the obvious solution is to perform a clean install of the operating system. Whilst this is a great solution, it is unlikely to work every time. It really depends how advanced the skills of the troll/hacker are with the piranha. One of the biggest problems with the clean install solution is you are playing into the exact game the piranha and the hacker want you to play. When a clean install is performed, all evidence of crimes and misdoings will be erased. This allows the piranha and the hacker to start the cycle all over again. It is a rinse-and-repeat scheme.

Another area of concern with this solution lies in the malware the hacker has installed on the computer. My hacker enjoys using early 2000s computer worms. These are nasty worms; technology and time have faded them away, but the piranha has made them very relevant again. In return, the worms have made the piranha much more powerful and indestructible.

The clear favorite of my troll/hacker is the Devnull worm. This worm primarily targets Linux operating systems; more recently, it has infiltrated Windows operating systems. Throughout the years, I have seen this worm attack my computers over 50 times. Within approximately 60 to 90 seconds, this worm attacks everything inside the computer. Pop-up after pop-up comes and goes from the screen within seconds, one after another, until the Devnull worm attacks every single file inside the computer. A clean install tends to calm the worm down—or maybe erase the preset code—but it never completely leaves the computer. Therefore, a clean install will erase crimes and misdoings, but the worm remains. The worm sits and waits for its next order from the troll and the We.piranha.

Narrowing down the worm entry point, Teredo tunneling opens the evil wormhole for Devnull and friends. Teredo tunneling, named after a marine mollusk called a shipworm which burrows into wood, is a legitimate networking protocol. It enables IPv6 connectivity over an IPv4 network; thus, the piranha uses the Teredo tunnel to access IPv6 networks even when the only connection present is an IPv4 connection. This allows the piranha's worms to tunnel past network security and attack.

Whenever I see the We.piranha send the Teredo protocol, it feels as if I am watching the Ghostbusters movie as the Ecto-Containment System(ghost-retaining machine) shuts down. All the ghosts fly out, run around wild, then attack me and my devices. This is the same thing in this instance with the worms. The tunnel opens up and all the worms squirm out, scurry around, then spread their slimy little malware all over my computer; all the while running crazy in the wild abyss of my hard drive. This is another form of legitimate technology the piranha has made evil by ever-evolving and adapting.

Fortunately for us, there are ways to fight these worms and other malware the piranha has released inside the computer. When dealing with the We.piranha and computers, we have to take the good with the bad. It is always one step forward and two steps back with the piranha; hence we must hurt ourselves in order to fight—toe-to-toe—in the computer.

—Note—I cannot even begin to say how many times I was forced back to factory, by the We.piranha, trying to find this solution. It was extremely difficult to hold my composure and allow my troll/hacker to continue to breathe.

A very direct path to fight the piranha in the computer is through the firewall and/or antivirus, but this path will not work. The We.piranha has every capability of operating as a fully functional master Xfinity/Comcast device. This allows free passage through any and all firewall and/or antivirus program without being flagged.

As we search for another path forward, there is an alternative way to fight the piranha in our computer. It is a pain in the neck, but then again, everything we do against the piranha is a pain in the neck. Therefore, we have to play the piranha's game—by our rules!

The hacker and the We.piranha's game is to send all of their worms, malware, protocols, etc., through PowerShell and Command Prompt. Notedly, we must block/disable PowerShell and Command Prompt, thus sticking a dagger into the gills of the piranha, preventing access. Luckily for us, this will be an on-and-off, permanent non-permanent situation.

There are two ways to accomplish this goal. We can prevent the protocols and other misdeeds from reaching the computer by blocking/disabling them in Group Policy Editor or Registry Editor.

—Note—I watched several online(anti-hacking) videos trying to resolve my situation with the piranha. These videos express quite a few preventative steps and measures the victim can take to protect themself, but none of it helped me, against the piranha. The hosts were extremely informative, but they were trying to prevent the average hacker; alternatively, we are dealing with evil like no other—a troll with the We.piranha. The online videos discuss disabling one or two settings, but we must look at the bigger picture. We must block/disable the whole thing: Group Policy Editor.

As stated, Group Policy Editor is capable of performing the preventative task we need, but there is a problem with Group Policy Editor. It is a hacker's dream and a favorite for the piranha as well. The We.piranha uses this editor to override antiviruses, firewalls, computer settings, and much more.

For this reason, we must not use it. Unfortunately, we cannot delete Group Policy Editor, as the piranha will reinstall it. Therefore, it must be blocked/disabled.

—Note—This is true for any program the piranha is using to hack the computer. The compromised program cannot be deleted. To prevent reinstallation and further misuse, each affected program will have to be blocked/disabled.

With such being said, we will block/disable Group Policy Editor the same way we block/disable PowerShell and Command Prompt. We will alter the piranha's games and block/disable all three through Registry Editor.

—Note—If the thought of blocking/disabling these three makes you sick, you are not alone. It made me sick too; however, this is what we must do to fight the We.piranha. We hurt ourselves to stop the piranha. Group Policy Editor and PowerShell are more heavily used, than Command Prompt, by the piranha. This is because they are a more efficient way of hurting the victim and the computer, as well as an easier way to send worms, malware, protocols, etc.

The Registry Editor provides us what we need. Plain and simply we need to fire back at the We.piranha and the troll/hacker. We do this by altering the registry keys. Be careful whilst altering the keys. If the keys are altered in an incorrect fashion, or the wrong keys are altered, severe issues can arise within the computer. These issues might even cause a—forced reinstall—of the operating system, hence use caution.

The specifics of the necessary steps to take will vary based on operating system. Subsequently, you must first determine which operating system the computer is using. Once known, search online for a step-by-step guide of the pertinent system, detailing the correct way to block/disable Group Policy Editor in the Registry Editor. Use the registry keys specified to achieve this goal. I prefer to block Group Policy Editor everywhere the Registry Editor gives me the option. Once finished, attempt to open Group Policy Editor to ensure it is fully blocked/disabled.

We will perform the same task for PowerShell. We need to add or edit the registry keys of the relevant section. Be mindful, these keys will be in a different section, and/or location, than Group Policy Editor. There are multiple PowerShell's(e.g., PowerShell, PowerShell ISE, etc.) needing to be blocked. As before, the best solution is to block/disable as many entries of PowerShell as can be found. Once finished, try opening all PowerShell programs ensuring it is 100% blocked/disabled.

Finally, perform the same actions using Command Prompt. Take the necessary steps and alter the registry keys in a prolific fashion. Unlike the last two, Command Prompt will only be blocked/disabled in one location within the Registry Editor. Now we will verify Command Prompt is blocked/disabled by attempting to open the interface.

—Note—If you wish to unblock/re-enable any of these, and use them again, the complete opposite will be performed. Once you have finished your task reblock/redisable them again. FYI, when you reblock/redisable them, nothing will be saved within the computer program. I would not recommend unblocking/re-enabling Group Policy Editor or PowerShell. It severely damages the ability to use the computer to the fullest extent. However, they must stay blocked/disabled to keep the piranha at bay.

Command Prompt is regarded different. Unblocking and using Command Prompt at times is a necessary task we must use to our advantage whilst fighting both the piranha and the troll/hacker. Command Prompt helps us inspect information about the computer, connections, attached devices, and other important details.

It is important to mention the Group Policy Editor helps the troll rain down and unleash his—hand of God—acts and tactics against us. Meanwhile, PowerShell allows the troll/hacker to send everything he wishes, with ease. Due to the extreme laziness of most trolls, we bring this up now. Also, be on the lookout for the echo command. Most commonly used in PowerShell, it is also present in Command Prompt. This command is considered lazy security and is often misused by hackers. If you have a piranha problem, most likely echo command is being used against you and your computer too.

Consequently, this is why we only block/disable Command Prompt in one location within the Registry Editor. The troll/hacker prefers PowerShell, thus we make it easy to re-enable Command Prompt.

The We.piranha loves to bypass the above tasks by downloading and installing Group Policy Editor, PowerShell, and Command Prompt in the format of a portable program.

Portable computer programs are programs/applications which can be used with various computers. They are not tied to just one computer, such as the normal version of the same program—instead, they are written on USB drives. For this reason, the troll/hacker, using the piranha, favors these portable programs as an alternative. Even when these applications such as PowerShell are blocked/disabled in the Registry Editor, the portable version of the same program remains accessible. Therefore, we must seek an alternative solution.

We could block/disable these portable programs by restricting the USB in which they are written, but this solution poses a significant challenge—it is extremely difficult to identify which USB to block. On my computer, the correct USB is labeled with a series of random numbers and letters, making it nearly impossible to pinpoint.

Portable applications can also be blocked/disabled through the computer's firewall settings. Some antivirus programs have application blocking features as well. In retrospect, we cannot use this solution as the We.piranha can manipulate firewall and antivirus programs with ease. The piranha uses and misuses them as if they were nothing, gobbling them up as if they were small shrimp on its way toward its ultimate goal—fully encompassing your computer.

A more plausible solution is to completely block all portable applications. This will be achieved through the Registry Editor, the same way we blocked Group Policy Editor, PowerShell, and Command Prompt. Follow the necessary steps outlined online altering the portable program registry keys along the way. Try opening up a portable computer program to test if you were successful. Portable computer programs can be re-enabled—just as before—if you wish to use them yourself. Remember to disable them again when you are finished.

—Note—There is no built-in setting in Windows to block/disable portable programs/applications. When altering the keys in the Registry Editor, you may need to create your own registry keys. Use your best judgment and do not be afraid to write the keys. Remember, our ultimate goal is to make the piranha—pound sand.

The steps mentioned above are the most effective way to protect your computer and kick the troll down the hill. Alternatively, you could take a more indirect approach by disabling certain settings, features, media, and so on, one by one, as you try to kick the troll. I tried this solution, but my troll would simply move on to the next way—and the next way—as if he were an energizer troll.

If you choose to disable one by one, there are recommendations as a starting point—file and printer sharing, Windows Defender SmartScreen, anything peer(to peer), and anything virtual-related. However, as mentioned earlier, in this method, disabling one by one might work for a while, but as the troll/hacker advances the ever-evolving piranha flourishes.

The piranha thrives on exploiting features, settings, and protections which are meant to safeguard our computers—against the computer. It is disgusting and annoying we must hurt ourselves to accomplish the main objective, but everything about the piranha is disgusting and annoying. Adapting to the codswallop the piranha spews toward us is the only way to keep up with the ever-evolving hacking device known as the We.piranha.

Whilst protecting the computer, just like everything else pertaining to the piranha, sometimes there does not have to be a logical reason why the hacker breaks in as much as he does—attacking the computer. Sometimes he breaks in—to the computer—purely for the love of being a troll!

—Note—I have been fighting the piranha, inside my computer(s) for over five years. Throughout this journey, I have used drastic measures, and the steps outlined in this method represent the best—computer—path forward I have discovered.

—Method 12—

—VPN Fighting—

Discussed earlier in the trick section, it is necessary to revisit VPNs here in the method section. If you suspect the piranha has infiltrated your VPN, there are a few ways to test the waters. Disconnect from your VPN then reconnect; this usually resolves the problem. An alternative is to switch your VPN program altogether. If you play around with VPNs enough, you will discover which VPNs the We.piranha has the hardest time hacking.

VPNs are also an excellent place to fight back if you suspect you are having Voice Over Internet Protocol(VoIP) issues. When dealing with VoIP, change your VPN regularly. Do not stay connected to the same VPN for too long.

Another way to fight back through your VPN is to go to the—VPN and Device Management—section of your device. In here completely remove(only remove from this section, do not remove the app) any and all VPNs listed. Removing them from this section will not remove the app, but it will remove the knowledge your device has of the app. You have now erased all history of the app in your device. Each time you change your VPN, use this to erase the one(s) you are not actively using. Now you can re-allow whichever app you choose, giving you a fresh start with each VPN. Only use one VPN at a time. If you have more than one listed in the—VPN and Device Management—section, delete(from this section only) the one(s) you are not using.

One last tactic you can use here, which I perform multiple times per day, is reset your network settings. This option is located in your settings tab. Depending on your manufacturer, you will have to look up, on the internet, exactly where in the settings it is located. This clears the congestion in your device. You will not lose any data as this only resets the network settings.

However, there is one point worth mentioning. When you reset your network settings, it automatically enables Wi-Fi. This may not be a concern if you are using a device which requires a Wi-Fi connection, but for cellular phones, this is a problem. If we can stay off Wi-Fi, we must, and the We.piranha tends to struggle when the personal network of a mobile device is used; we must use this to our advantage. Meaning do not use a wireless internet connection with your cell phone. Use your cell phone's own cellular data connection. Finally, on rare occasions, resetting the network settings does enable Bluetooth. Be cautious of this situation and if it happens, turn Bluetooth to the off setting.

Resetting my network settings always seems to annoy my troll, in turn. it makes me feel like I just drop-kicked the piranha out of the water. It will come crawling back, but this definitely helps and is a must in my arsenal, whilst fighting the We.piranha.

Take these new VPN skills and expand your thoughts to fight back with all your might. You have now grasped the essence of my knowledge of—VPN fighting!

—Method 13—

—Court Fight—

Going another legal route, you can use the court system method. Fighting your troll/hacker and the We.piranha in court is very painstaking and daunting but if you win, it is also very rewarding.

More than likely, your troll/hacker has been performing some form of surveillance on you and your property. In the unlikely event they have not, they are still using the We.piranha to hack into your internet and your life. When the piranha steals your personal information and attacks you, this is thought of as a form of virtual rape and virtual stalking!

I would not even know where or how to begin a legal matter regarding virtual rape. However, I can say you do have the legal right to file a Civil Stalking Injunction. This process, though, is quite difficult. You must follow the guidelines in your local jurisdiction and file everything perfect. There is little room for error.

Given your troll has possession of the piranha, it is likely he also has a better financial situation. Whether the troll funds come legally, or illegally, these are the cards you are dealt.

I would like to share how things went for me in this situation, allowing you to make your judgment and choose accordingly. Make the decision whether or not this court path will work for you.

—Example—

I felt trapped with no other route to take. The local police department was worthless, and Xfinity/Comcast refused to help me. Everyone, including both these entities, kept telling me I should go to the local courthouse and file a Civil Stalking Injunction. I kept asking the same question to both of them—why would I go to the courthouse, and file a Civil Stalking Injunction, when you are the police? When you are Xfinity/Comcast? Every time, the only answer I received was—we do not know how to help you!

In return, I would cuss and see red, usually storming out of whichever building I was in at the time. Shake my head, kick my truck, flip off the cops, and a bunch of other irrelevant stuff, then I finally decided to file a Civil Stalking Injunction against the neighbor to the West. There were close to 36 codes broken and over 8,000 breaches of my internet per day coming from my hacker and the piranha.

It was tough, but I won the Civil Stalking Injunction. To no avail, it did not last long. My troll filed for an evidentiary hearing. He hired a fancy attorney, meanwhile, I represented myself. I had no money because my troll and his wife(troll two) had stolen everything I had. During the hearing, he lied over and over about irrelevant actions and the judge ate it up! On the other hand, my troll/hacker did admit to many things, including stalking, hacking, and stealing from me.

Subsequently, I did not see a reason to show evidence if my hacker was admitting to the accused actions. The judge stated since there was no evidence(I had evidence, but the judge did not ask for it, and there was no reason to show it), the court was letting the accused perpetrator go free, and the Civil Stalking Injunction would be dismissed. I kept my cool as I was railroaded in the courtroom.

I left the courthouse in disbelief at the outcome of the hearing. All I could think about was being railroaded, and this was a bunch of horse feathers, to say it politely! When the troll/hacker came home, he started hacking more and more, taking more videos and pictures, and spotlighting my house.

After much resistance from the judge—and I mean much—I was able to get a second Civil Stalking Injunction granted. Then my troll/hacker was able to get another evidentiary hearing granted. I thought to myself, this is so ridiculous. Here we go again. This time my plan was to show any, and all evidence I had, no matter what happens.

In a strange twist of fate, this is where the story ends. The email communication amongst myself, his attorney, and the court staff stalled out completely. I really do not know what happened. I would send emails, and neither his attorney nor the court staff would reply back to me. His attorney would email the court staff, and they would not get back to the attorney. Although extremely unprofessional, it did not matter to me. I already had a valid and current Civil Stalking Injunction.

The We.piranha hacking never stopped during this whole court matter. Before, during, after—it did not matter, as the tenacity of the piranha continued.

A Civil Stalking Injunction is just a piece of paper! I heard this saying many times before, and I did not believe it, but this day the statement was proven true. There is a high probability if you go to court against your hacker and you are granted a Civil Stalking Injunction, you will end up with a prioritized, worthless court document—just like me. If you get a Civil Stalking Injunction granted, and your troll/hacker stops the piranha attacks, thank God! I am proud of you, and I am happy for you!

Here is one final positive way to look at the situation. Whether or not the hacker continues or stops—a granted and current Civil Stalking Injunction does open the door to file in court for monetary gain.

—Method 14—

—Terminate the Internet—

This is not the last method we will try, but this certainly is one of the more drastic methods we will try. Every fishy situation is unique; thus, every fishy situation will vary. First, I must remind you, the whole time I fought the We.piranha, I was an Xfinity/Comcast customer. Knowing this might help you brainstorm ideas whilst you battle your troll with the fish. I think having Xfinity/Comcast most likely makes hacking with the piranha easier for the perpetrator, but I am positive, in the long run, it does not matter. Keep this in mind as you read this method.

Jumping right in the water, if you have Xfinity/Comcast, call them on the phone. Give them the bird through the phone(of course), tell them—take it on the arches—then disconnect your services. After much dismay from ten different people, in ten different countries, your Xfinity/Comcast services have now been terminated and you are free and clear of the We.piranha—or are you?

Unfortunately, this is not the end of this method; this is only the beginning. Watch your devices and your network for the next few days to see how things pan out. When I finally terminated my services, it felt as if I just gut-punched the tummy of the troll. I definitely think it hurt him, and hindered the piranha, but I quickly realized my paralyzing tactics had worn off and he was hacking away, again!

If your internet services are through a different provider, choose what you believe is your best path forward. Have confidence every decision you make is the right decision. My years of fighting the We.piranha have led me to believe it can breach any provider; therefore, I personally would terminate my services.

Moving on, if terminating your services has solved your piranha problems, then great! Congratulations!

On the other hand, the rest of you must keep fighting. Try disconnecting the internet connection entering your house. This is different than disconnecting it from the wall socket of a room in your house. The idea here is with the cable disconnected(to the house) there will be no possible way for any type of internet connection to travel into your house. This may or may not work, as it depends on how determined your troll/hacker is with his piranha.

Our last resort in this method—cut the cord, literally. Everyone has heard this term. We will now put words to action as we cut the cord. One end is attached to the telephone pole and the other end to your house. You will want to make a cut at both ends of this cable.

Let me explain how this whole situation played out for me. Follow my example in relation to your real-life situation.

—Example—

I called Xfinity/Comcast to terminate my service. After much agony and dismay, I was finally able to cancel all internet service. Obviously, I hoped this would stop the piranha from extending its reach inside my home. Obviously, I was wrong. I did not notice a difference at all. Deep down, I wanted to believe things had changed, but they had not.

The first two days after terminating my services I did not share my feelings, regarding the status of the piranha, with my wife. When I finally did share my feelings, we both decided it was time to cut the cord. We had already disconnected the cable from the outside of the house; hence cutting the cord was the only option we had left.

I grabbed my ladder and climbed onto the roof. Knowing I was probably being watched, my plan was to play coy with a decoy. As soon as approached the cable connected to my house, ironically on the same side of my house as the troll/hacker—I was spotted. I nonchalantly knelt down next to the rain gutter, all the while picking up globs of dirt and debris from the gutter, throwing them down on the grass. I did this for about 60 seconds until the troll finally turned his back to me to get a drink of soda pop.

It is now or never! This should be fun, I thought to myself. I reached down, placed my needle-nose pliers around the wire, and cut it. I hoped things would get interesting, but even I was in for a surprise. The troll/hacker turned around as the wire was falling to the ground, his jaw dropped just as fast. Meanwhile, I felt extremely accomplished. I was smiling. I flipped off his house. I thought things were going well.

I climbed down from the roof, grabbed my ladder, and made my way to the other end of the wire—the part attached to the power pole. I set my ladder up in the bumpy grass, then climbed as high as I could go on the ladder. I reached up, cut the cable, and left as little as possible dangling from the power pole(FYI I figured the least amount of cable left on the pole, the better).

Ten minutes later, the local police were at my front door. My troll/hacker filed a false police report! He claimed I had been climbing and crawling on the roof of his garage next to the power pole. This was simply not true and completely absurd.

It turns out the reason my troll called the police was because the piranha was still able to hack my house through the attached cable, even without internet. Once the cable was cut, it hindered his ability to steal and hijack my services via the piranha. What services? I do not know! Electricity? Cell phone data? These are the mysteries of the piranha.

Anyway, my troll/hacker wanted the police to arrest me for cutting a cable he alleges we both use(attached to my house only). He also wanted Xfinity/ Comcast to come to my house and reconnect the cable at my expense! I told the cops the neighbor was a jackwagon and I do not agree to those terms. Take me to jail for destroying my own property! Yeah, not going to work with me! After a while, the police left. I do not think they like me, but I am fine, I do not like them either!

After everything was said and done, it took my troll/hacker two days, and the hacking via the We.piranha was back in full swing. I hope cutting the cable works for you, and I hope my example helps you in your situation. Keep in mind, in my opinion, I am dealing with one of the most determined hackers—not just in America, but the world.

—Method 15—

—Beat up the Troll/hacker—

This method might seem a bit barbaric, maybe even a little drastic. I understand many of you may not be the fighting type, but if pushed far enough, everyone has their limits.

There is one thing this whole situation has taught me. I would love to beat the living shit out of the troll/hacker controlling the piranha attacking me! It is very probable you feel the same way about your troll/hacker. The obvious solution, go kick his ass. In my mind, this solution has always been foreshadowed.

However, the problem with my situation is the troll/hacker of my We.piranha attacks is a coward. If your troll/hacker is a coward too, this method will not work for you. Do not do anything to gamble your freedom. No trouble is worth an assault charge—or possibly even worse. Extremely tempting, but going to prison will not solve anything.

Instead, we must call him out for a fair fight—well, a fight with the least amount of repercussions. Right now, the coward is coming out of the troll; we must switch it around and bring the troll out of the coward!

How does this help our We.piranha situation, you ask? I would say several ways. Best possible solution is the troll/hacker stops the piranha attacks. Hopefully, they at least slow down; ergo maybe this criminal, whom you hate, decides to move. Lastly, if nothing else, at least it feels extremely exhilarating to beat the shit—or try to beat the shit—out of your troll/hacker.

If you try this method, remember a few small unwritten rules to follow—never go to the den of evil to battle your troll. This means never go to his property to fight. If you go to—troll—property, he could claim trespassing or he was taunted, scared, etc.

This rule boils down to the fact you cannot trust a thief, liar, hacker, etc. Consequently, we must either go to neutral ground or remain on our own property to fight. A possible alternative would be to let your troll/hacker punch you first, then strike back, adamantly claiming you were defending yourself.

I tried the—beat-up-a-troll—route somewhere between 30 and 50 times. I felt as if I was playing Wack-a-Mole, but I could never wack the mole. Most of the time when I called my troll/hacker out, he would say going to the sidewalk, or my property, was too far to walk. Laughable, yes...true, also yes!

The rest of the time, he would bark and make wild, rabid hyena noises. I really do not know why he did these things. He was not mentally challenged; I mean, after all, he is a top-five hacker in the world. He was just mentally unstable.

Do not shoot your troll/hacker unless you absolutely have to shoot him. For the love of God, try not to shoot him! Because of this whole We.piranha situation, I now carry several weapons at all times whilst on my property. My troll/hacker has already paid someone to break into my house at least once, I foreshadow at least once more soon.

Shooting and killing my troll has crossed my mind over 100,000 times, but it is simply not worth it. Reiterating, going to prison will not solve anything. Remember this whilst you battle your troll.

The beat-up-a-troll method can vary depending on whether or not you are battling a male or female troll/hacker. Use your best judgment and do not engage in anything resulting in unnecessary trouble for you. This is very difficult under the circumstances, but keep your wits about you all the while carrying yourself in a manner demanding authority.

Lastly, if you are battling more than one troll/hacker, and it is a male/female combination, beating up the male troll might make the female troll stop as well. Do not feel sorry for either one of them. Do not feel sorry for kicking their asses or anything else for this matter, as they do not feel sorry whilst violating you.

—Chapter 6—

As time has progressed, we have covered numerous ways to battle the We.piranha. Through thick and thin, come hell or high water, some evil piranha schemes remain unchanged.

This section of the book discusses ideology and concerns not fully addressed elsewhere in the book. Keep your eyes open and watch your surroundings like a hawk. The piranha goes against all known forces. There are still some things we are yet to find a relevant answer/solution.

In light of these forces, a section dedicated to preventative tasks has been created. They represent problems we must stay vigilant for in our journey. The tasks below do not belong in the method section, but I have provided some advice where possible. Small steps may help prevent the piranha from causing larger issues down the line.

—An ounce of prevention is worth a pound of cure—

—Preventative Task 1—

Large waves of noise, or disturbances, are constantly sent—from the piranha—to the victim's house. These waves are most likely caused by either Electromagnetic Interference, Harmonics, or Spurious Emissions.

Electromagnetic interference(EMI), harmonics, and spurious emissions are related concepts in the field of electrical engineering and electronics, but they are not the same thing.

Here is a breakdown of each term...

EMI—broad category encompassing any electromagnetic noise which affects electronics.

Harmonics—specific types of electrical disturbances tied to waveforms in power systems.

Spurious Emissions—refer to unintended signals produced by devices which can interfere with other systems.

Whilst they can all contribute to issues in electronic devices and systems, they arise from different phenomena and are generally addressed through different means.

Most noticeable whilst watching television, or listening to the radio, these waves affect everything in the victim's household. All high-voltage and all low-voltage devices are impacted—the piranha spares nothing! It can even cause lightbulbs to flicker.

—Preventative Task 2—

The We.piranha executes mass data transfers. These are different than simply movies being downloaded or online gaming. Research suggests these transfers are primarily conducted for identity theft and espionage purposes. These mass data transfers are very important to try and decipher. Much of the transfers come and go via email using Dovecot—widely used mail server software.

—Preventative Task 3—

The Piranha steals power. This is happening through the waves of noises and/or disturbances and through the mass data transfers. The main meter of the target house is impacted as well. To reduce impact, try placing tinfoil on the entire plastic face area of the meter. At least three layers of tinfoil, but five is preferred. FYI, this did not work for me, but it may work for you.

—Preventative Task 4—

Most hackers prefer to attack with worms rather than viruses. This is also true with trolls and hackers controlling the We.piranha. They love using worms to attack their victim. Worms spread extremely quick—replicating code—without human intervention. The piranha spits out worms, everywhere inside a device, creating immediate impairment.

Some of the more common worms the piranha uses include Devnull, Hiupan, Prometei, and Quad 7.

Devnull worm—designed for Linux, but more recently found on Windows Operating Systems as well; this worm compromises the host, then downloads and executes an extremely quick and devastating shell script from a web server.

Hiupan worm—software associated with China-based espionage actor Earth Preta AKA Mustang Panda.

Prometei worm—AKA Prometheus, is a botnet—modular—worm meant to mine cryptocurrency for the hacker and the We.piranha.

Quad 7 worm—AKA 7777, is a botnet worm which steals credentials in password spray attacks. This worm also targets VPNs and routers.

The piranha enjoys using Teredo tunneling. The worms mentioned above gain entry to the victim's device through these tunnels. Once entry is gained, the piranha cripples the device, rendering its use nearly impossible. When the hacker sends these worms, they are committing severe computer crimes against you and I. Watch for these types of worms entering your devices. Most commonly seen in computers, these worms have also been spotted in cell phones, tablets, and other devices. Remember to document everything whilst protecting your devices.

—Preventative Task 5—

By all accounts, the We.piranha has the capability to crypto mine. The doors are open, and the piranha is sending the Prometei, AKA Prometheus worm, to crypto mine the victim's device. Other ways exist for the piranha to crypto mine devices, but this worm has been the prevalent and preferred choice for my troll/hacker. Crypto mining is very important to monitor, as the troll/hacker behind the piranha is very much a thief, looking for an easy payout.

—Preventative Task 6—

Another way for your troll/hacker to manipulate you and your devices is through Ethernet over Power. Many people use this extended network technology and the piranha loves to take advantage. The Quad 7 worm also assists the piranha in this venture. Additionally, the We.piranha turns the tides by using Power over Ethernet against the victim. Ethernet over Power, and Power over Ethernet both mean exactly as their names imply.

—Preventative Task 7—

Do not leave credentials stored on any device. Whilst removing credentials might seem like wishful thinking in the fight against the piranha, we must try. The more ways we safeguard every element of our lives, the more we can reduce the impact of the piranha.

The same element applies to network connections stored within devices. Any device deemed—not internet necessary—should have the saved internet information removed, immediately. If a device is connected via Ethernet, then Wi-Fi is not necessary, and vice versa; thus remove one or the other. Do not leave both enabled, as this keeps the watergate open for the piranha to come inside your machine.

—Preventative Task 8—

The We.piranha can attack anything with a computer chip. The voltage does not matter; everything is fair game.

To prevent as much damage—and theft—as possible by the piranha, unplug everything. Do not simply turn off the power to each device or the power strip. Every unnecessary device must be unplugged from the wall outlet. Only leave essential devices plugged in. When needed, plug in the necessary device, use it, then unplug it again when finished. The piranha knows everything with power in the target house. This includes vacuums, radios, and other battery-operated devices.

—Preventative Task 9—

Remove batteries from all laptops. Do not leave any power, whatsoever, to any computer when not in use. If a computer is shut down, but still has power ran to it, the piranha can hack and attack the machine. At times this is difficult for non-hackers to comprehend, but it is true and it must be addressed.

Subsequently emphasized, unplug all computers from the wall socket when not in use. Remove all batteries from all computers when not in use.

—Preventative Task 10—

Most computers have a CMOS battery. It keeps the system clock running and BIOS settings intact when the computer is off. The We.piranha has the capability to drain this battery, causing additional annoyances for you and I. A computer can run without a CMOS battery, but it will lose BIOS settings each time it is powered off. This leads to longer boot times and potential configuration setting loss. If you notice your CMOS battery draining when it probably should not be draining, the piranha is the likely culprit.

—Preventative Task 11—

Large quantities of telemetry are sent nonstop, from the We.piranha, to the victim's computer. This telemetry allows the piranha to steal from and spy on the victim. To achieve these goals, the piranha sends out phishing messages to devices. The common piranha tactic is steal the identity first, go phishing second. Check all your accounts regularly, including banking and utilities. There is no known way to prevent the piranha from phishing, but the damage can be mitigated.

—Preventative Task 12—

Hackers controlling the piranha use various techniques to hide the execution of mass data transfers by the We.piranha. One common method is through steganography. Using the practice of steganography, secret piranha messages can be concealed within other seemingly harmless messages, files, images, videos, audio, and more. The We.piranha uses Baseline DCT and Huffman coding to encrypt and hide the deceitful information. Depending on the knowledge of the hacker, the steganography most commonly embeds within JPEG and PNG files. Be vigilant for steganography on your computer.

I have never been able to crack the messages on my computer, as they are encoded too well. If the steganography messages—unwillingly bestowed upon you—are cracked, you might be able to answer every question you have about the whole We.piranha situation in your life.

—Preventative Task 13—

Along with the steganography, the piranha leaves documents everywhere within computers. Whilst some are encoded, others are legible. In a way, they are leftover debris. The troll/hacker does not want the debris on the computer, but they cannot stop it from happening. It just goes where it goes, or ends up where it ends up. Most of these are written documents—or formats—of the codes and protocols being shouted out by the piranha.

The best practice is to sift through these garbage documents. Try deciphering everything occurring within the computer. File viewer and editor programs can be downloaded to make these documents easier to read. If you cannot find the documents on the computer, try using a recovery program to look for lost or deleted files. Do not forget hidden drives, including USB. With enough computer knowledge, one might be able to use these documents to their advantage.

—Preventative Task 14—

Cover all webcam lenses on computers, televisions, tablets, and other necessary devices. The piranha thrives in voyeurism. It can install virtual webcams without the victim's knowledge.

In a similar fashion, disable volume on all computers. Volume is an extremely sought-after and commonly used entry point for hackers.

—Preventative Task 15—

The We.piranha has the capability to attach Bluetooth devices to cell phones and tablets. Many times these Bluetooth devices stay hidden from common technology. Apps can be downloaded to help locate these leeching Bluetooth devices.

—Preventative Task 16—

Free local television, which still relies on antenna signals, can be widely accessed within a household. However, the piranha can intercept this free connection, hijacking the signal and enabling mass data transfers through the lines. As a result, the victim is left unable to use their free local television.

—Preventative Task 17—

Extension cords should never be used whilst fighting the We.piranha. The clear advantage for the piranha is the connection. The joint causes cameras and other devices to malfunction.

—Preventative Task 18—

Pay attention to other active devices. By this I mean helper devices. As powerful as the piranha is, there is always room for other devices. Be observant of named switches and access points, likely operating side-by-side with the piranha. This includes virtual and physical. They should be visible in a list of network connections on a computer. They could also be seen in the trees or wires above the troll/hacker(s) house or your house.

—Preventative Task 19—

The piranha has the ability to limit the use of websites, including access to government websites. The hacker can pick or choose, then program, which websites one can or cannot use/visit.

Walking the same line, it can also see open webpages. These pages are visible, to the piranha, on any device. Keep this in mind as you surf the internet.

—Preventative Task 20—

The We.piranha knows which devices are connected to the internet at all times. Be cautious whilst using hotspots. The piranha knows when a personal hotspot has been opened and can manipulate them. It steals everything about the hotspot, including data. Upload and download speeds will drop significantly as the piranha steals everything.

—Conclusion—

Knowing the preventative tasks listed above should help guide your journey. Even though many of these tasks have no definitive answers, bringing them to your attention is critical. Many other We.piranha tricks, methods, and preventative tasks do exist. The ones listed in this book are the main ones I am knowledgeable toward, hence attention is emphasized.

—Epilogue—

The We.piranha is in a merry-go-round cycle of vicious torture against the victim. This cycle must end for everyone.

With over five years of torture, closure will be coming with a very steep, bittersweet price. My wife and I invested 10 years of heartfelt love into what we believed was our forever home. Sadly, there is no way to preserve this life, or home, anymore. A fresh start is necessary, as our forever home has been turned into a for-never home again. We realize the only way we can truly ever—break free—from the piranha or the troll is to move to a new state.

With this move, the end of the piranha's cycle of torture will hopefully come fast for me. I wish I could provide a definitive answer, pinpointing exactly how to fully win against the We.piranha. The truth is, there are no winners in this battle. I lost more than I will ever recover. So much has been stolen—financially, mentally, physically, and in terms of my sense of security.

The one thing I will finally regain is my freedom. My freedom not only to live again, but live free of the We.piranha. In America, we are born into what is supposed to be the land of the free. The piranha, and my troll/hacker(s), stripped this right from me.

The wrath of hell and fury the piranha brings leaves this cycle open to begin again, with a new victim. As the cycle starts anew, so lies the We.piranha for the next target. A new round of theft, lies, and military deceit will bring new questions for new people, but this will no longer be me.

The most logical questions regarding the We.piranha will likely never be answered. Victims of the We.piranha must keep faith and never lose hope for resolution. Every tunnel has a light at the end, and this tunnel is no different.

A new day will dawn, bringing the light at the end of the tunnel closer and closer. Whilst the threat of the piranha will always be there, the steps outlined in this book turn the tide against the piranha. We all wish and dream the We.piranha(e.g., .off, .xb6, etc.) will one day be out of our lives forever. I hope now there is a path forged ahead for all of us!

Wishes and dreams will always be wishes and dreams unless we make them a reality. The reality of this situation is the piranha is better suited in our past than our present.

—Veni Vidi Vici—

www.ingramcontent.com/pod-product-compliance
Lightning Source LLC
LaVergne TN
LVHW090428210926
848480LV00002B/732
* 9 7 9 8 2 2 7 2 0 9 9 9 3 *